HARDPRESS.NET
HOME OF HARD-TO-FIND BOOKS

European Acquaintance
by J.W.De Forest

EX LIBRIS ESCORNALBOU

EUROPEAN ACQUAINTANCE:

BEING SKETCHES OF

PEOPLE IN EUROPE.

BY

J. W. DE FOREST.

AUTHOR OF "ORIENTAL ACQUAINTANCE," &c.

NEW YORK:

HARPER & BROTHERS, PUBLISHERS,

FRANKLIN SQUARE.

1858.

CONTENTS.

A

EUROPEAN ACQUAINTANCE.

CHAPTER I.

FLORENCE TO VENICE.

PURSUED by the fretting enmity of a monotonous invalidism, I one day reached the triple saloon, the white pillars, and the marble-covered tables of the Café Doney in Florence. I was hob-a-nobbing with Galt, the sculptor, over a couple of ice-creams, when my companion looked up from his spoon, and addressed an individual who stood before us with a "Good evening, Mr. Greenough."

I rose and shook hands with a gentleman of agreeable air, though reserved and commanding, whose features were high and fine, whose eyes were of a stern gray, and whose full beard and mustache gave him all his natural grave manliness of aspect. Drawing a furred glove from his white taper fingers, Greenough sat down by us, and began to urge me with his rich voice and earnest manner to exchange the warm breezes of Italy for the cool waters of Graefenberg. Hydropathy, he thought, was the temple of health, and, Priessnitz was its high priest, or rather its deity. He had spent eighteen months in the establishment at Graefenberg, beholding in that time marvelous cures, not on strangers only, but also on members of his own family. So fervent was his faith, that I finally accept-

ed it as my own, and was persuaded to look for my
lost health in the rivulets of Silesia, as Ponce de Leon
sought his departed youth in Floridian fountains.

In the person of Neuville, a Virginian looker-on in
Florence, and also a sufferer from some of the chronic
flagrancies of nature, I found a fellow-traveler and co-
disciple in hydropathy. When we bade Greenough
good-by, he gave us a letter of introduction to Priessnitz. Thanks be unto the merciful angel who veils
from us futurity! for it would have been a sombre
parting had we known that we were never to see this
fine artist and gentleman again. Before I returned to
Florence, delirium and fever had torn his cunning
hands from the marble, and swept his poetic spirit
away to other visions than those of earthly beauty.

Through Bologna, Ferrara, Pavia, glancing from the
prison of Tasso to the banquet-rooms of Este, from the
chamber of Parasina to the dungeon of Hugo, from
wonder-halls of painting to cathedrals of aged solemnity, we passed over the mountains and the broad, rich
plains which separate Florence from Venice. A rail-
road station now puffs its disrespectful smoke inter-
mittently over the lagoons which glitter around the
dethroned Queen of the Adriatic, and makes itself especially ridiculous by reminding the traveler of Vesuvius breathing out its fire and vapor over the Bay of
Naples. It was twilight by the time we got out of
the cars, and dim evening before we emerged from a
passport-office looking toward the distant lights of
Venice. Gondoliers bellowing from black gondolas
wanted to carry us to the city, like undertakers with
floating coffins desirous of conveying us to some sea-

deep cemetery. There was at first a contest among these amphibious gentry as to whether we should take a gondola or an omnibus; but, unable to agree among themselves, or perhaps out of sheer good-nature, they finally left the matter to our decision. When I tell the poetic reader that we selected the omnibus, he will probably sniff with contempt and resolve to cut our acquaintance. But let him grant us his patience; we had financial reasons for our choice: we were as hard up for cash as Mother Hubbard's dog for a bone. Having miscalculated traveling necessities at starting, our united pockets now contained the residuum of one zwanziger, or about fourteen cents. We might have flourished our letters of credit, to be sure; but the gondoliers would have understood their value as little as that of the belles-lettres. The 'bus was half price; the 'bus, we thought, would roll us straight to the hotel; and so, in sultry disappointment, we declared for the prosaic 'bus. Off went our trunks with the agility of chairs and tables under the influence of old witches or modern spirits; and, struggling after them through the noisy, eddying crowd, we reached a long covered boat, which looked as much like a gondola as a horse looks like a pony.

"Enter, gentlemen, enter; take your places under the canopy," said the master boatman, pointing with a warning finger to heavy clouds floating low in the twilight air. We got in cautiously, as people get into all tight places, knocked our knees together, knocked our hats together, and took the latter off.

"This isn't an omnibus," said Neuville, looking me gravely in the face at the distance of six inches.

"No; but I suppose we shall find it on the other side of the ferry, if this is a ferry."

"But what if we have to pay the ferry extra?"

"Can't do it.   That's their look-out.   We must tell them they should have thought of that before, and have arranged matters better for gentlemen who only had a zwanziger."

Such was our desperate conversation, while trunks and individuals were being rammed into our pen until we were as close as little pigs riding to market.   The boatmen took their places, and we glided out of the turmoil of gondolas, gondoliers, passengers, and policemen.   Night had fallen by this time, sullen and starless, changing Venice into shapeless masses of shadow which sat mysteriously on dusky waters.   A pattering of rain-drops, the monotonous dip of paddles, quick cries of men who passed us unseen like warning but invisible spectres, were the only jarrings on the wonderful silence.   We knew that we were threading the avenues of a great city, and therefore the darkness appeared more ghostly, the stillness more supernatural; therefore did it seem as if we were traversing no city of upper earth, but rather those " caverns measureless to man which run down to the sunless sea."   Through the Grand Canal without knowing it, between rows of lofty palaces without beholding them, under the Rialto without a consciousness of its shadow, we passed noiselessly, blindly, like those who are ferried over the river of death.   I felt a vague melancholy, an ineffable sorrow stealing over me, as if I were riding as chief mourner at my own funeral, and wondering whose turn would come next.

"It seems to me that it takes a great while to get to the omnibus," was my remark.

"I don't believe there is any omnibus," replied Neuville, with the indignation of outraged good faith.

Presently the bow of the boat grated against some stony obstacle, and we became conscious that our watery bier had ceased to advance.

"Behold us arrived," said the boat-master. "Behold the Albergo d'Europa."

I crushed my hat in the little doorway, straightened myself up, and bounded on to a broad flight of steps wet with the rippling of the canal. Above me rose gigantic stories of a palace front fretted with columns and pilasters, and casting red glares of light outward through deep windows and open balconies. Before it slept sombre waters, flickering here and there under lamp-flashes or the sparkle of a lost star-beam, and spreading solemnly away into an intensity of darkness and mystery, from some unknown shore of which shone other lights, as of fairy islands unattainable by human presences.

"Is this the hotel?" I questioned.

"Yes, gentlemen," responded a head-waiter in a white waistcoat; "this is the Hotel of Europe, at your service."

"But where is the omnibus?" was the inquiry of my undiminished perplexity.

"You have just got out of the omnibus, gentlemen. That boat there is the omnibus."

"Oh," said I, turning to Neuville, "I thought that was the omnibus all the while."

"Of course you did," replied Neuville, scornfully;

A 2

"it looks as much like an omnibus as an alligator looks like an elephant."

Having stared anew at the maritime vehicle, we told the waiter to pay for our passage, and walked into the hotel, wiser than before on the subject of omnibuses.

I have no intention of describing Venice at length, inasmuch as it has been visited by other travelers equally well provided with Murrays. We sailed in gondolas, visited the Arsenal, made an excursion to the Lido, paid a boatman to sing Tasso and love-songs under the Rialto, and did various other things appropriate to the locality. We likened the fretted architecture of the palaces to a filigree of marble; Saint Mark's, with its many domes and colors, to a mass of gigantic bubble-work; the rich canvases of the Venetian painters to gorgeous sunsets hanging in the walls of the west; the black gondolas, vanishing down watery avenues, to hearses borne along the dim naves of mighty cathedrals.

THE ISLAND CITY.

The midnight mariner with wondering eyes
    Beholds a city on the Adrian waves,
Whose palaces from ocean depths arise,
    Like saintly shining souls from earthly graves.

The moonlight glorifies its vaulted fanes,
    Its proud pavilions and its dizzy towers ;
The lamplight from its archéd windows rains
    Along the sea in ardent, trembling showers.

No whirring wheels, no clanging coursers sweep
    Beneath the shadows of its princely piles ;
But sombre barks, inaudible as sleep,
    Glide down the silence of sea-paven aisles.

FLORENCE TO VENICE.

Discovered through its air of lucent balm,
   Though near, it seems mysterious and far;
Its life is beautiful, unearthly, calm—
   An angel city of some sinless star.

So shines that splendid city of delight
   Which poets build on Fancy's magic surge;
Yet richer far, more delicately bright
   Than cloud-wrought cities on the sunset's verge.

Most musical the sea around it chimes,
   Responsive to the mind-harps in its halls;
Most fragrant breezes from all starry climes
   Uplift the standards on its shining walls.

And poet souls in barks of amethyst
   Sail down the ripple of those tides of love,
And feel their foreheads gently crowned and kiss'd
   By unseen angels bending from above.

O joyous palaces! heroic towers!
   O trustful oratories! yearning spires!
Seraphic limnings, fervent-hued as flowers!
   Eternal sculptures, passionate as fires!

Who leaveth earth? Who voyageth with me?
   Who lifteth sail in Poesy's rich air,
To search Imagination's wonder-sea,
   And find the poets' Island City there?

CHAPTER II.

IN VENICE.

ABOUT a week after our arrival in Venice, while patrolling the colonnades of the Piazza San Marco, Neuville and I met a couple of fellow-countrymen, Irwine and Burroughs, Southerners, whom we had previously seen at Florence.   As we had a stomach apiece, all empty at the moment, we adjourned for conversation to a restaurant handily situated in one of the palace-fronted edifices which, on three sides, confront and ennoble the piazza.

" We are going to Graefenberg," said Neuville over his macaroni *à la Milanese.*

"We are going to Graefenberg," echoed Irwine over a glass of *vino rosso.*

" We shall take the cure," continued Neuville.   "I suppose you try it also."

" Not a bit of it," replied Irwine.   " Priessnitz will have to talk himself to death before he inveigles me into his tubs.   I know all about those water privileges."

" Oh, you have been through the mill, then ?"

" Not such a blockhead, if you please.   But I have seen other people in the suds, and was satisfied with the simple spectacle.   I went to an American watercure with a friend, and was incautious enough to stay over-night.   They stirred me up in the morning, and decoyed me, while I was half asleep, into a wet sheet.

I got out of it as quick as I could, and went off at a
canter, in hopes of getting warm once more in my life.
Came to a spring at last, among the brushwood; a
little dirty spring, with footmarks in the mud all about
it.   There was a sick minister and his wife, with their
tin cups in their hands, looking at the spring and looking at the mud.   The minister was very small in the
legs and very much wrapped up about the head; gave
a fellow the idea of a fork standing on its tines.   I
thought of two chickens on a frosty morning staring
at the snow, with one leg tucked up among the feathers.   At last we all stepped gingerly into the mud,
like cats, drank more than we wanted, and went off up
the hills in very low spirits.   When I got back to the
house, I found the little minister and his wife, as chilly
as ever, surveying the breakfast table.   It was a long
pine table without any cloth, a row of white plates set
like buttons along the edges, with pieces of brown
bread and tumblers of milk between them.   'My dear,'
says the minister, 'it looks like a very cold breakfast
for such a sharp morning.'   'Oh dear me!' says she,
'I suppose it's good for us.'   I ate what I could get,
and then took the first conveyance out of the place.
So, you see, I know what you fellows are coming to.
I prefer to die without suffering so much.   You might
as well kill a man outright as starve and freeze him
to death."

At the expiration of a fortnight in Venice we went
to the police-office to demand the right of departure.
All over Italy, excepting perhaps Piedmont, the police
have the same troublesome habit of taking away a traveler's passport when he enters a city, and obliging him,

if he stays over a week, to procure what they call a *paper of residence*, or *paper of surety*. At the end of his sojourn he swaps off his *carta di residenza* for his passport, gives a little something to boot most probably, and is allowed to go in peace. I knew very well of the existence of this unprofitable custom, but somehow forgot it at Venice, and so never applied at all for the said residential papers. Accordingly, when Neuville and I appeared at the police-office, and quietly demanded our passports without any thing to exchange for them but our forgetful heads, the officer nearly burst with wrath and astonishment.

"How!" he thundered, nearly petrifying us with the ferocity of his green spectacles; "no paper of residence! I should like to know what this means. How dare you live a whole fortnight in Venice without a paper of residence?"

We explained to him that we did not know what it meant ourselves; that we did not dare to live so any longer, and that we wanted to get away and go somewhere else as soon as possible. He seemed utterly dumbfounded by our apologies, and indeed by the whole circumstance, which was perhaps unparalleled in his official experience, and was certainly a stigma on the police of the city. He gave us the passports, however, after shaking his head at us long enough to upset his brains, and perhaps went addle-pated before bedtime under the belief that the world was full of Yankees who had no papers of residence.

We were rather lucky in getting off with so little trouble. Had we been Englishmen instead of Americans, we might have gone farther and fared worse;

that is, been turned out of Austria altogether, or, possibly, expressed on to some unpleasant Hungarian prison. Perfidious Albion was just then in great disfavor with the góvernment of the Cæsars, which accordingly delighted in entangling and thwarting those traveling Britons who happened to touch its mighty spider-web of watchfulness. An amusing Irishman named D'Arcy, whom I met at Dresden, related to me how he had a difference of opinion with the Venetian police concerning his projected journey from Venice to Vienna. "We can not give you a permit to go to Vienna," said the official; "we shall make out your passport for Milan."

"But I have just come from Milan," returned the surprised D'Arcy. "I have seen Milan, and seen it enough."

"Very possibly; but we want you to go back there. It is extremely suspicious that you are so anxious to go to Vienna."

"Not at all. I want to go to Vienna because I want to see it. Every body wants to see Vienna."

"But what makes you so resolute to see Vienna? What is your particular motive—your object?"

"Oh, I want to see it because it is such a beautiful city, and because it has such beautiful palaces in it, and because it has such beautiful women in it. Every body tells me about the beautiful women there; and, begging your pardon for taking such a liberty, I shall die if you disappoint me."

The official looked monstrously puzzled, for every one was on the broad grin, and a certain suspect Hungarian was treasonably enjoying himself in a hearty

laugh behind his traveling cap.   At last he ungraciously appended his valuable autograph to the passport;
and the dear, darling D'Arcy, as his friends called him,
went off triumphantly to see the pretty women of
Vienna, among whom, as I afterward heard, he made
no trifling sensation.

"I must tell you, by the way, of a dispute that I
had with a countryman of yours," said D'Arcy to Burroughs and myself.   "I was sitting in an Italian hotel, close by a party of Americans, when one of them
declared that Old England was nigh her downfall.
'I'll take you up on that,' said I.   'I'll meet you,' said
he.   So we had it there, back and forth, for an hour
together, without convincing each other a particle.   He
gave me his card when we separated.   His name was
Greeley, and I heard that he was the editor of a large
New York paper."

"Greeley!   I'm glad you pitched into him," said
Burroughs, who hated England himself, but who, as a
Southerner, hated Greeley more.

Returning to my subject, I observe that stories in-
numerable might be collected of ludicrous encounters
between travelers and the Continental police, especially
that of Austria.   The broad brims of wide-awakes have
repeatedly afforded a spacious battle-field for these two
antagonistic classes of society.   A friend of mine journeyed in one of those revolutionary head-dresses from
Florence to Vienna without molestation; but it was
not permitted that he should brave the Austrian eagle
in its nest with impunity, and that watchful fowl made
a triumphant peck at him when he least expected it.
Taken into custody in the street by a spy in citizen

costume, aided by a couple of soldiers, he was marched to a police-office, with the proof of his political turpitude on his devoted head. The chief of the office got into a fearful rage at sight of him—not so much because of the hat, as because it was late, and dinner was waiting. They were about to secure the government for one night against the seditious broad-brim by locking it up, and locking its owner up with it, when a friend, who had witnessed the capture, arrived with a *valet de place* from the hotel just in time to make explanations, and save our countryman from repenting of wide-awakes in the night-watches of an Austrian prison.

" It was all a mistake, then ?" asked the officer.

" Oh ! quite a mistake."

" You had no evil intentions in wearing a broad-brimmed hat ?"

" None at all ; not an intention in the world."

" Well, go then. But buy another hat. Do not be seen again in the streets with such a hat as this, or the consequences may be very serious."

My friend bought a steeple-crown before breakfast the next morning, and thus, for a second time, was the Austrian empire saved from destruction.

A farce on the same subject as the above was played at Milan, partly in my own presence. Presenting my passport at the police-office of that city, I met an English acquaintance, a capital fellow named Budd, who, with a look of brazen impenitence, was receiving an admonition concerning the radical character of his hat. " Good-morning, Signor Budd," said the officer from behind his desk, leaning forward, and looking search-

ingly, though civilly, into the broad, handsome, good-
humored, but determined face which confronted him.
"We sent for you, signor, to speak to you about
your hat—the one you have in your hand at this
moment."

"It is worthy of the honor," said Budd; "it is a
good hat." And he held up the battered, dusky-white
broad-brim with an air of affectionate admiration.

"Precisely, signor; very useful, I have no doubt.
But it may bring you into trouble. You are aware,
doubtless, that its form and color are both unusual;
you are aware that hats of that species have been the
badge of a certain disorderly and treasonable party.
You have also a full, long beard, which is equally a
badge of the said party. The whole marks you as
singular, and attracts an unpleasant degree of popular
notice."

"But," responded Budd, "I am not an Italian. I
have nothing to do with Italian politics. I wear such
a hat and beard as suit my style of beauty and my
notions of convenience."

"Exactly, signor. You have nothing to do with
politics; we know it well. We know all your tastes
and all your haunts. You went into the country
yesterday. You were at the *Café delle Colonne* the
evening before. You were at the house of Signora
Bellina the evening before that. You have been
watched ever since you reached Milan, and we could
tell you where you have been and what you have done
on every single day. We now know that you are not
a dangerous individual, and we wish to persuade you
to avoid the appearance of being such. We have no

intentions against your beard, signor; you are welcome to keep it. But we would counsel you to discontinue wearing that hat: it would be so easy to lay it aside, and might save you so much trouble."

"Very well," said Budd; "but, if I am to change my dress at the suggestion of the government, I want some particular directions as to the new style which I am to adopt. Just give me a written order specifying the kind of hat which I am to wear, and I am ready to obey it. But I must have the order. I want to send it to England; it shall be published in *Punch* or the *Times*. I could get five pounds for such a paper in England."

The officer was nettled, and looked angrily at the row of white teeth which glittered maliciously through Budd's black mustaches. Controlling his temper, however, he went on with his admonition, although not in quite so composedly gracious a tone as before. "Signor, we can not give you such an order; it would be absurd. We leave the matter to your own sense of propriety and your prudence. But what we specially complain of is not so much the hat itself as your manner of wearing it. You wear it turned up, and turned down, and twisted, and cocked, in a style which attracts a great deal of attention, and is particularly obnoxious."

"Oh, I wear it according to circumstances," said Budd. "I will explain all that to you (sticking it on his head). Now, when the sun is on my right, I turn it down so (hauling the right brim down); and when the sun is on my left, I turn it down so (a haul at the left brim); and when I want to take a general view

of the country, I turn it up all around (brim cocked
up throughout its entire circumference); and when
the wind blows, I slap it down on the top for safety
(a smart pat on the yielding crown).

"But just give me an order *how* I shall wear my
hat. It would be better than the other. The *Times*
would give me twenty pounds for such a document as
that."

"Signor," said the officer, losing all patience, and
beginning to stammer, "you will find, perhaps, that
this is no jesting matter. You had better consider it
seriously, and answer us seriously. We are advising
you what is for your own good, and what may save
you a great deal of annoyance. Think of it again,
and see if you do not come to our opinion."

In short, they had a long, and, in part, a rather
stormy discussion, some of which I heard, while the
rest Budd related to me afterward. In the end, he
had the moderation to take the officer's advice, and
lay aside his wide-awake while he remained on Austrian territory. It is a fact that the obnoxious head-
dress excited no little popular attention; all the more,
doubtless, because it shaded keen black eyes, a jetty
beard, and a visage remarkably Italian in feature.
People stopped to gaze at him as he passed along the
streets, and gathered round him by the dozen when he
halted before any object of a tourist's interest, staring
with an earnestness almost of expectation, as if they
saw before them Mazzini or Garibaldi about to cry,
"*Viva la repubblica!*"

It is small consolation to the traveler who is pestered by these impertinent regulations to observe that

they fall with double force upon the natives. It makes
him indignant, rather, to see a foreign yoke lying upon
so fair a country, so nobly fashioned for empire, and
to see the sons of that country so slavishly submissive.
But, on the other hand, he can not help acknowledging
that in hardly any other similar expanse of Italy is life
so respected, property so safe, and land so well tilled
as in the Austrian Lombardy. The people are governed sternly, but not stupidly; they are not allowed
to think for themselves, but they are encouraged to
work for themselves; and this is not visible certainly
under the Italic rule of Pio Nono and King Bomba.
Venice is, indeed, decayed and decaying; but such
must have been its destiny, no matter who were its
rulers; for its riches and power necessarily flew away
on the vanishing wings of its commerce; and the
Austrians are hardly more responsible for its decline
than for the fall of Babylon or the death of the first
Cheops.

CHAPTER III.

VENICE TO GRAEFENBERG.

A TOLERABLE steam-boat carried us to Trieste, which I observed to be a newish city, affluent in ships and store-houses, and lively with a rapid circulation of dust and people about its broad streets. In freshness, movement, and an appearance of growth, it reminded me of Marseilles, and even of sea-port towns in my own flourishing country.

Coming in late at night, we got so little sleep that it was hardly worth taking, and by ten in the morning were bundled off in a rickety, uncomfortable omnibus for Vienna. A few hours of leisurely ascent brought us into one of the most beautiful highland districts in the world, full of abrupt turfy hills, rocky precipices, dells spotted with thickets, lucent rivulets, endless diversifications of feature in short, all shaded into fine variety by an abounding verdure of dark, tapering firs, exactly suited in color and contour to the Alpine character of the scenery. I would describe this lovely land more minutely, but that I was crushed by sleep, and rode through a large portion of it with closed eyes, and mouth perhaps open; so that I have only an indistinct recollection of its sharply-sketched landscapes, as if I had seen them through a mist, or a pair of some grandmother's spectacles. Once, as my head jolted about unpleasantly, I partially awoke, and stuck it through a strap which depended from the roof of the vehicle for the support of passengers' elbows. There it hung an hour or two, like a head cut off for a trophy, until I aroused thoroughly, and wanted it again to look out of the window.

We reached Laybach, changed our abominable diligence for a rail-road car, and thenceforward journeyed most comfortably. On the way we learned that Radetzky, the victor of Novara, the greatest living general of Austria, was in the train with us, hastening to a convention of the Austrian, Russian, and Prussian monarchs at Olmutz. At Gratz, a fine large city, the station was surrounded by an extremely well-dressed multitude, with many beautiful women in its ranks, all eyes and mouth to welcome the great man. Presently there rose a shout, signifying that he was visible, and we leaned out of the windows to share the spectacle of heroism in a white coat. A very little old hero he was, with very white mustaches, very sore eyes, and a very wizened appearance generally, as if much dried up by the hot fires of musketry to which he had been exposed. After standing a moment in full view on the platform of the car, he caught hold of the iron guard and made a little boy's jump to the ground. There was a great hurrah, as if the Gratzonians were delighted beyond control to see him keep his legs without assistance. I felt no inclination to quarrel with them on the score of their enthusiasm, for Radetzky is said to be as kind-hearted as he is brave, able, and energetic.

They have good hotels at Vienna, glorious coffee, bread unequaled otherwheres, and the most artistic soups. We were strengthening ourselves in the eating saloon of that most recommendable house, the Römischen Kaiser, when we were addressed by a stranger, a tall, genteel, middle-aged man, with a newspaper in his hand, who was lounging near us at a table from which the remnants of his dinner had just been removed. "Excuse me, gentlemen," he said in good English, marked by only a slight foreign accent, "excuse me for interrupting you; but I see that you are Americans, and I am most happy to meet you. I have spent many years in your country, and always feel, in addressing an American, as if I were speaking to a compatriot. Still, I am a German; not an Austrian, however, but from Baden. I must observe, notwithstanding, that I am acquainted in Vienna—widely acquainted. Allow me to ask if you stay long here."

"Only a week, probably," said one of us, while the others stared in wonder at this outpouring of courteous communicativeness.

"I am sorry for that, as I should take great pleasure in presenting you to some of the first classes here," continued our magnificent friend. "I have many acquaintances among the upper ranks of society here, who would be most happy to receive any of your countrymen introduced by me. By the way, I am surprised that so few Americans ever select Germany as a place of residence. There are in the United States many families, with moderate incomes, who could make their means go much farther and include many more luxuries here than there. Baden, for example, would be an admirable place of residence. A court, if you care for such things; a very respectable theatre; an

Opera even; baths and society; galleries and universities better than your own, within easy reach; all, too, at a wonderfully small expense. An American family might live there comfortably, educate its children thoroughly, learn French and German well, and amuse itself very pleasantly, for less money than it would cost it to live at home unamused and only half instructed."

In this politely patronizing style our friendly unknown discoursed for half an hour, and then, with elegant sadness that he should probably see us no more, took his departure. "What do you think of him?" said one. "He is a humbug," said another. "He is a spy," said a third. "He is a professional gambler," said a fourth. Young America, it must be observed, was in this case quite young, for which reason it flung out its verdicts with a vigor amounting perhaps to uncharity. Yet it had reason for its suspicions: it was in a land tainted with espionage; in a community broken out with *rouge et noir*. Unknown, too, in Europe, is such hospitable confidence as this, of introducing to the best society strangers who bring no other recommendation than the cut of their coats and faces.

The German is acquired with astonishing facility, and Neuville proved it. Irwine, the only one of us who had any previous intimacy with that tongue, went to the principal theatre to hear a German tragedy. Neuville accompanied him—not with any Babelish fancy of listening to an unknown speech, but to get an idea of the arrangement of an Austrian theatre, and the appearance of a Vienna audience. On their return they were in a state of equal enthusiasm as to the excellence

B

of the scenery, the power of the actors, the ingenuity of the plot, and the sublimity of the language.

"Why, good heavens, Neuville," said Irwine, "what in the world did you understand?"

"Oh," replied Neuville, with infinite gravity, "I heard some fellows saying '*Mein Gott!*'"

We spent eight days among the galleries, churches, palaces, gardens, and promenades of Vienna, all of which time my great hurry to reach Graefenberg compels me to bury in oblivion. Once more on the rail-road, we never halted until we were in Herrmanstadt, a village some thirty miles short of our moist destination. It was Saturday night when we landed at the little hotel on the public square, and we spent Sunday in staring at the huge boots and gorgeous short petticoats of the peasant bucks and belles. As Irwine and Burroughs still hesitated about taking the cure, we sent for the landlord, and questioned him concerning Priessnitz's reputation in the surrounding country. He did not know; he could not say any thing certain; Priessnitz had cured some people and hurt some people; but he had a friend who had been there, and would tell us all about it.

In the evening came his friend—a tall, thin, long-nosed young German, who spoke English comprehensibly, having learned it, as he said, from his British fellow-patients at Graefenberg. With the universal good-humor of his countrymen—the most obliging set of mortals under the sun—he sat down to a pipe, and told us all he knew about hydropathy and its results. "You can go if you like," said he, "but I advise you no. You will stay there long time and think you get better, but you will be as the first day, but worse; and all the time you think you get well the next day. I stay there eighteen months, and then I ask Priessnitz why I am not better, and he say that I stay not long enough; but I say that I stay too long, and I come away. There are some peoples who think they are cured, and go away and get back all their maladies. Nevertheless you can go and try, but I think you will find it as I say."

Thus he went on for half an hour or more, murdering our language and our hopes in the same breath. He was so evidently sincere and well-informed that he nearly converted us to despair, and made the faces of Neuville and myself in particular look as long as rope-walks. We thanked him heartily for his kindness, although it nearly killed us; and he went away, charitably wishing us a better streak of luck than he had found himself. After his departure we talked up our courage again to a moderate height, and finally bade the landlord arrange for transporting us to Graefenberg the next morning.

A green, rolling, woodland country, the eminences of which steadily heightened as we advanced, was the scene of our day's journey. It drew toward evening when we found ourselves rolling through the long winding valley in which stands the little borough of Freiwaldau, and above which towers the hill of Graefenberg. A vagrant rivulet touched at intervals upon the road side, chilling us already with prospective baths in its swift and frigidly crystalline waters. Here and there stood linen factories, around which bleached long strips of cloth, stretched out like immeasurable recum-

bent ghosts on the emerald meadows. What a provi-
dence, I thought, that the great water-doctor should
have been born in a country where he could so easily
supply himself with douches and bandages! As we
neared Freiwaldau, the road was lined by cunning little cottages, built roughly of hewn logs, but blooming
through every window with pots of flowers. It astonished me to see this poor and uneducated peasantry
thus adorn its dwellings with those simple beauties
of nature, which our better-fed and better-schooled
laboring classes of New England usually neglect, if
they do not coarsely despise.

Rattling into an open square, with a town-house in
the centre, encircled by the more aristocratic buildings
of Freiwaldau, we pulled up at the Golden Star, obtained rooms, sent for the landlord, and instituted new
inquiries concerning the success of Priessnitz in killing
or curing his patients. But here Priessnitz was taken
for granted—Priessnitz was an axiom, an admitted fact.
The only point on which our host differed from the possible opinion of the great man was in a certain theory
that his hotel was a much better place of residence
than the Establishment. The lodging was wretched
at Graefenberg, he said; the food was worse, and the
building had a bad odor. As to ablutions, he would
order a tub big enough for us all, have a bath-man
come to the hotel to superintend our moistenings, and
provide us with as much water as four reasonable mer-
men even could desire.

The Golden Star was a pleasant planet enough, and
some of us were disposed to accept its head-angel's invitation; but Irwine, whom the air of the locality had

already fanaticized, declared for Graefenberg, no matter how disagreeably musty; so that we finally resolved to visit the Establishment and smell it for ourselves, before we rejected the privilege of living under the immediate wing and cluck of Priessnitz.

CHAPTER IV.

INSTALLATION AT GRAEFENBERG.

THE whole landscape was buttered with sunshine when we sallied out to climb the long hill, half way up which shone the whitewashed walls of the great Silesian Water-cure. It was, nevertheless, the weather of a belated spring; so cool that we covered ourselves against its breath with our winter overcoats. I will also remark (begging the public's pardon for mentioning such a thing) that we were, one and all, stoutly underclothed with flannel; and I wish particular notice to be taken of this fact, as it is of considerable interest when taken in connection with the butterfly costume in which we fluttered about a few days afterward.

Through streets of solid stone-and-plaster houses we passed into a narrow sweep of meadows, and crossed a lively brook of clear water, variously useful in washing invalids and dirty clothes. In the shop windows were displayed huge brogans, stout canes shod with iron, drinking-horns, and pretty cups of Bohemian glass, all significant of the teetotal peripatetic society into whose haunts we were about to venture. Half way up the hill we came to a little fountain, where a solitary individual was swallowing water with an air as if he thought very small beer of the liquid, but supposed it was good for him. Some hundred yards farther on was another costive fountain, dripping from the base of an obelisk of gray stone, on which shone the inscription, "AU GÉNIE DE L'EAU FROIDE."

From here onward we met numbers of people of a cheerfully crazed appearance, wandering confusedly hither and thither, like ants when you scatter their nest, all of them shabbily attired—some in linen, as if in derision of our flannels; some bareheaded, with clipped hair, others with towels about their temples—their pockets bulky with glass cups, or their shoulders harnessed with drinking-horns. Most of them carried thick canes, and raced up the eminences with the hearty good-will of Christian climbing the hill Difficulty. Ladies, too, were visible, shoeless and stockingless, wading through the dewy grass, their feet burning with what Doctor Johnson would have called auroral frigidity and herbiferous friction. They all kept in constant motion, and seemed never to speak to each other, reminding me of those bewildered knights in Ariosto's enchanted palace, who wandered perpetually up and down, hearing the voices of dear friends, but seeing no one. The centre of movement for this distracted crowd was an irregular square, stony and verdureless, on one side of which rose two enormous ghastly buildings, with multitudinous windows, constituting the establishment proper; while opposite these, at various distances, glared low, whitewashed cottages, also used for the stowage and cleansing of a vast invalidism. From a concave in the masonry of the outer stairway to the principal edifice gushed a hearty little jet of water, abundantly supplying the horns and cups which were continually presented to its humid mouth.

Priessnitz was absent for the nonce at Freiwaldau;

but a bathman led us to the superintendent of the Establishment.   Entering a side door, we mounted to the dining-hall, with our handkerchiefs to our offended nostrils; for the landlord of the Golden Star had not misrepresented the perfumes which haunted the building. Our first supposition was that these smells arose from decayed patients, who had got water-logged and mouldy from having been kept too long under treatment; but our guide through this rancid region favored us with a more humane, and, as I afterward discovered, a more probable explanation.   In Silesia, as in Syria, the natives still preserve a venerable custom, derived, I presume, from Noah's ark, of uniting stable and dwelling-house under one roof.   The Arabs, indeed, keep hogs out of their cellars, and are not apt to overcrowd them with cows and calves; but the Silesians despise or ignore these fastidious precautions, and consequently our noses were in great indignation.

Bare, creaking stairways and floors brought us to a prodigious desert of an eating-room, varied by an oasis of table (land), and scattered with caravans of unpainted chairs in lieu of camels.   The superintendent, a short, flabby man, with a baldish crown, an apple-dumpling face, and white eyes, came to receive us.   I have forgotten the exact price which he demanded for board and lodging, but it was something extremely insignificant; not more, certainly, than three dollars a week. It was so much like gratuitous hospitality that we sent a porter to the Golden Star for our trunks, and followed the superintendent to one of the cottages.   We found it a very rustic one, built of raw clapboards, and approached through a puddle, the overrunnings of a neighboring water-trough. It had begun life, indeed, as a stable; but we objected very little to that, as the scent of quadruped life had been totally exorcised from its breezy chambers. The floors and partitions were of the consistency of pasteboard, and we saw at once that, if we did not wish to disturb our neighbors, we must live in a whisper. Every thing was of unsophisticated pine: the walls, the narrow bedsteads, the chairs, and the aguish wash-stands.

There were only three chambers for four of us, and but one of them was double-bedded and double-chaired. We tossed up kreutzers for the single rooms. Irwine got one of them, and Burroughs the other. While the trunks were coming we commenced a dance in celebration of our advent, thinking that, perhaps, we should never feel like it again. Presently we heard a yell of fury from some profundity below, accompanied by a double knock against the floor under our feet from what seemed to be a pair of boots. We paused in our Shaker exercises, questioning what abodes of torture might exist beneath us, and what lost mortal or demon might inhabit them. We afterward found that a neuralgic Russian lived on the first floor, and that, feeling annoyed by our clamor, he had sought to mend matters by howling and throwing his shoe-leather about.

Presently we all gathered in the passage to catechise a young Englishman who was also (in)stalled in our ex-stable. Having been three months under treatment, he could give us some idea of what we were to do and to suffer; but, in the very middle of his talk, he was imperiously summoned away by a moist, cool executioner, armed with a wet sheet. In a moment more we heard, with mingled mirth and horror, the rasping splash of the dripping linen as it fell upon our friend's devoted body; and, a quarter of an hour afterward, we saw him hurry out, with wet locks, and make off, at a shivering canter, for the mountain paths.

By half past twelve we were bearing our empty, expectant stomachs up and down the great eating-hall. Patients followed patients through the creaking doors until nearly two hundred sick, blind, and deformed people were hungrily patrolling around the long tables. Eight or ten neat, curiously white-faced damsels hurried in and out, loaded with piles of plates, or with monstrous loaves of what seemed to be mahogany bread. Presently they all entered in a column, bearing spacious, smoking platters of meat and vegetables, prepared, as I afterward found, by cooks of Satan's providing. No other signal was necessary to the famished invalids, who immediately made for the tables at a pace which reminded one of the fast-trotting boarders of a Western hotel. However sick they may have been in other respects, they were certainly well enough to eat; and I think I never saw, before nor since, such an average large appetite among such a number of people. A disgracefully dirty man, with an ugly, swelled face, who sat on our left, filled his plate three or four inches deep with every kind of provender, ate it up, and then did it again, and a third time, as if it were no feat at all. We afterward learned that Priessnitz counseled his patients to eat all they wished—the more the better; for the old peasant was as perversely ignorant of a stomach as if he carried a crop and digested with pebbles, like a chicken; maintaining, among other heresies, that a water-patient's gastric powers should be strengthened by hard digestion, as much as his legs by hard walking. Partly in consequence of this monstrous theory, and partly because of the native savageness of Silesian cookery, the food was of the worst description, consisting of such horrors as veal ten days old, sauer-kraut, and the most unsusceptible dough-balls. Such a diet would produce a galloping dyspepsia in any one who was not invigorated by frequent baths and wet rubbings; but, as things were, I imagine that no great harm was done, and that, in a general way, two hundred ostriches could not have digested better. A man who takes four cold duckings per diem, walks five or six miles after each of them, and wears a wet bandage over his abdomen, may confide, even to recklessness, in his gastric juices.

When we came to discuss the dough-balls above-mentioned, a German astonished us by saying that they were the favorite dish of the Emperor Ferdinand of Austria. "Yes," said he, "with those they coax him to sign state papers. He is rather childish now, and thinks it a great bore to be always putting his signature to proclamations and treaties. Accordingly, Schwartzenberg tells him that, if he will write his name so many times, he shall have dough-balls for dinner."

Our meal closed with spacious fruit pies, not much less than two feet in diameter. All these indigestibles gave our stomachs exercise until six o'clock, when the table was set again with the fragments of the mahogany loaves, and pitchers of sweet and sour milk. At ten we went to bed, and discovered that we were expected to keep warm with one blanket apiece, although the weather was chilly enough to palliate the use of four. For fear of a wet sheet, however, or some other such cold comfort, we took care to call for no additional covering, and supplied the hiatus for the night with our plaids and overcoats.

CHAPTER V.

FIRST DIPS IN GRAEFENBERG

EARLY in the morning Priessnitz came into our room, followed by Franz, the bathman, and by Irwine, who lent himself as interpreter. I saw before me a medium-sized person, with weather-beaten features ; a complexion which would have been fair but for deep sunburn ; eyes of blue, inclining to gray ; thin, light-brown hair, touched in with silver, and an expression reserved, composed, grave, and earnest. He sometimes smiled very pleasantly, but he spoke little, and wore, in general, an air of quiet, simple dignity. Altogether, I felt as if I were in the presence of a kindly-tempered man of superior mind, accustomed to command, and habitually confident in his own powers. I afterward observed that he kept the same impassive self-possession in the presence of every one, were it even the highest noble of the Austrian empire.

He listened to a brief history of my malady, seeming very indifferent to its past symptoms, but examining attentively the color of my skin and the development of my muscles. He then ordered the wet sheet to be spread, and signed me to stretch myself in it. As soon as I had measured my length on the dripping linen, Franz folded me up rapidly, and then packed me thickly in blankets and coverlets, as if I were a batch of dough set away to rise. Neuville followed

my damp example, and our teeth were soon chattering
in chilly sympathy.   Having noted the intensity of our
ague, as if it were a means of judging what degree of
vigor in the treatment we could bear, Priessnitz marched off to survey the agonies of Irwine and Burroughs.
Neuville and I remained as fixed, and nearly as moist,
as King Log in the pond, but in a state of anguish far
beyond the capacities of that solid potentate.   We
were so cold that we could not speak plainly, and
shivered until our bedsteads caught the infection.
Then a change came—a graduated, almost unconscious change to warmth—and, at the end of ten minutes, it was hard to say whether we were uncomfortable or not.   A few minutes more brought a sensation
of absolute physical pleasure, and I began to think
that, after all, water was my element, and that it was
quite a mistake that I was not furnished with tasty
red fins like a perch, or a convenient long tail, for
sculling, like a polliwog.

Just at this pleasant stage of the experiment, when
I would have been glad to continue it longer, Priessnitz came back, and declared us ready for the plunge-
bath.   Franz turned up the blanket so as to leave my
feet and ankles free, shod me with a pair of straw
slippers, set me unsteadily upright, like a staggering
ninepin, took firm hold of my envelopments behind,
and started me on my pilgrimage.   I set off at the
rate of a furlong an hour, which was the top of my
possible speed under the circumstances.   Forming a
little procession, with Priessnitz ahead as the officiating priest, then myself as the walking corpse, and
then Franz as sexton, we moved solemnly on until

we reached a stairway leading into a most gloomy and low-spirited cellar. Dank, rude, dirty flagstones were visible at the bottom, while from an unseen corner bubbled the threatening voice of a runlet of water. The stair was so steep and the steps so narrow that it seemed impossible to descend without pitching forward; but, confiding myself desperately to the attraction of gravitation, I cautiously raised my left foot, made a pivot of the right one, wheeled half a diameter, settled carefully down six inches, wheeled back again to a front face, brought my dextral foot down, and found myself on the first step. Ten repetitions of this delicate and complicated manœuvre carried me to the flooring of the cellar.

Franz now engineered me into a side room, and halted me alongside of an oblong cistern, brimming with black water, supplied by a brooklet, which fell into it with a perpetual chilly gurgle. In a moment his practiced fingers had peeled me like an orange, only far quicker than any orange was ever yet stripped of its envelope. As I shuffled off the last tag of that humid coil, the steam curled up from my body as from an acceptable sacrifice, or an ear of hot boiled corn. Priessnitz pointed to the cistern, like an angel of destiny signing to my tomb, and I bolted into it in a hurry, as wise people always bolt out of the frying-pan into the fire, when there is no help for it. In a minute my whole surface was so perfectly iced that it felt hard, smooth, and glossy, like a skin of marble. I got out on the first symptom of permission, when Franz set about rubbing me down with a new linen sheet, still possessed of all its native asperity. If I had been a mammoth or an ichthyosaurus, with a cuticle a foot thick, he could not have put more emphasis into his efforts to bring my blood back to a vigorous circulation.   Priessnitz joined in as if he enjoyed the exercise, and honored me with a searching attrition from his knowing fingers.   Then, after examining me, to see if I grew healthfully rosy under the excitement, he signed me to throw a dry sheet over my shoulders, and give myself an air-bath before a window into which a fresh morning breeze was pouring.   Holding tight with both hands to the corners of the sheet, I flapped my linen wings as if I were some gigantic bat or butterfly about to take flight through the orifice, and soar away over the meadows.   "Goot!" said Priessnitz, nodding his solemn head in token of ample satisfaction ; and, folding my drapery around me, I marched up stairs, like a statue looking for a pedestal, or a belated ghost returning to its church-yard.   I met Neuville descending with a stiffness of dignity which made me think of Bunker Hill Monument walking down to get a bath in the harbor ; so woefully solemn, so dubious about his footing, so bolt upright and yet so tottering, that he would have shaken the gravity of a pyramid, or moved a weeping crocodile to laughter.   Once more in the double-bedded chamber, I gave myself a few hurried rubs of supererogation, and was about dressing, when Neuville and Franz reappeared from the lower regions.   With shivering fingers I seized my thick under-wrapper, and proceeded to don it, with a glorious sense of anticipatory comfort.   But that atrocious Franz saw it, snatched it, tucked it under his arm, made a grab next at my drawers and stockings, and then signified, by menacing signs, that I was to leave my cloak on its nail. No luckless urchin in Dotheboys Hall was ever stripped half so pitilessly. As for Neuville, who had been toasting himself over American fires through the mediocre chill of a Florentine winter, and was as sensitive to wind as a butterfly, or a weathercock, or Mr. Jarndyce himself, he was despoiled with the same hyperborean unkindness. Out we went, nearly as thinly dressed as Adam and Eve, but leaving no Paradise behind us; forth we hurried, driven by Franz, that bald-headed cherub, horribly armed with a wet sheet; away into the woods we fled, to wander like Cains, and drink three or four tumblers of water before we might venture back to breakfast.

I took my first taste at the House fountain, and swallowed a pint with difficulty. I seemed to be choke-full of water; oozing with it at every pore, like the earth in spring time; ready to brim over with it if I were turned ever so little off my perpendicular; fit to boil and steam like a tea-kettle, should I incautiously venture near a fire. It is astonishing how much moisture can be absorbed into the system through the skin; how nearly a man can resemble a water-logged ship or a dropsical cucumber.

It was a raw, misty morning, as are nearly all Graefenberg mornings, and the chill humidity crept like a breath of ice through our thin remainder of raiment. Loose and shaky, from our coat skirts to our teeth, we ambled up the hill back of the Establishment, in hopes of sheltering ourselves in its woods from an ill-dispositioned wind, which blows, year in and year out, over those unfortunate landscapes. People passed us or met us every minute ; some just starting out, in a state of aguish misery ; some returning, rosy and happy in their triumphant reaction.   The wide path, moistened here and there by spacious puddles, entered the forest, and wound gradually up the mountain.   At every hundred yards or so, smaller tracks diverged through the thickets, or a bubbling fountain reminded the passer that it was time to quench his thirst, if he had any.   There must have been twenty miles of pathway around Graefenberg, all, or nearly all of which had been paid for out of a small weekly tax levied on the patients.   Several score of fountains, some of them mere wooden troughs, others basins or obelisks of stone, had been erected by means of this same revenue.   Then there was a bronzed lion, and two other monuments of considerable cost, dedicated to the honor of Priessnitz, one by the Prussian patients, one by the Hungarians, and the third, I believe, by some German noble.

Now and then we found some favorite fountain surrounded by invalids, chatting cosily, or pausing to drain their cups, and reminding one of a parcel of hens clucking and drinking about a water-trough.   Neuville and I made a very respectable pedestrian effort that morning, and returned to the house with anxious voids in our stomachs, notwithstanding that we occasionally stopped to refill them with water.   I should have mentioned that Franz had surcingled us with broad linen bandages, of which the two first turns were wet, and the two last dry, so as to constitute altogether a kind of towel-and-water poultice.   This is the finest digestive aid or curative that I know of; as much superior to stomachic pills and cordials as it is nearer to nature.

Breakfast was on the table, as it had been for two hours, when we entered the eating-hall. Like the last night's supper, it consisted of sweet and sour milk, with the usual rye and barley bread. By the time we had swallowed a disgraceful quantity of this simple nutriment, our waist bandages were dry, and required a new wetting. Then we repaired to a booth and bought stout canes, with iron foot-spikes and curved handles, the thickest and fiercest that could be had. Then we debated whether we should get drinking-horns to wear over our shoulders, or drinking-cups to carry in our pockets. At last we decided in favor of the cups, and resolved to visit Freiwaldau after dinner, and choose some handsome ones of Bohemian glass. Then eleven o'clock arrived, and Franz had us away to sit face to face, for fifteen minutes, in tubs of cold water, at the end of which he polished us off with wet sheets in lieu of sand-paper. Then we got ashamed of the effeminacy of hats, and walked out conspicuously under bare polls and green umbrellas. At one o'clock came dinner, which gave us hard work in the digestive and peripatetic line for some hours afterward. At five, Franz wanted to put us in the wet sheet again, and would not take " no" for an answer. Then we had to walk half an hour or more to get warm ; and, by the time we returned, it was necessary to eat more sour milk and mahogany. Then we remoistened bandages, preparatory to trotting for an hour or two up and down the great, ill-lighted hall, in company with scores of other uncomfortable people. The room was naturally chilly, built so expressly and by malice aforethought, as I believe ; in addition to which, that rascally superintendent delighted in throwing open an elevated range of windows, thereby giving copious ingress to a damp wind that wandered among our shivering forms like the ghost of a wet sheet.   Nine o'clock sent Franz after us, who insisted on wetting our bandages and putting us immediately to bed, in as comfortless a state as half-drowned puppies.   Repeatedly in the night we woke, aching with cold, for our rations of bed-clothing were still restricted to a single blanket.   At five in the morning Franz was upon us, like the Philistines upon Samson, or like Samson upon the Philistines (for it seems to have been nip and tuck between those old fellows), dragging us down again into those awful nether regions of wet pavements, brooks, and cisterns.

It was astonishing how rapidly we became fanaticized under the influence of the cure and the example of our fellow-invalids.   Before a week was over I had discarded all my woolen garments of every cut, and wore linen from head to foot in a temperature like that of a New England March or a Charleston December. It blew every minute, and rained nearly as often ; yet we caught no colds, and were savagely indifferent to our discomforts.   All this, too, was in despite of sarcastic declarations, made on our arrival, that we would dress and behave like civilized people, and not like the slouching, bare-headed, bare-footed fanatics around us.

It was also remarkable how this general carelessness in exteriors depreciated the average beauty of the patients.   Among the five hundred persons who were under cure in Graefenberg and Freiwaldau, there must have been a number with some natural claims to comeliness ; but, by dint of shabby clothes, cropped hair, and neglected beards, this favored few had melted away into the great aggregate of ugliness, or retained, like Lucifer, only a doubtful halo of former beauty. One of our party, a man of sensitive nerves, complained that the daily spectacle of such a deteriorated humanity made him unwell, and that he never should convalesce until he could see some handsome people.

CHAPTER VI.

CERTAIN GRAEFENBERGERS.

NEUVILLE and I had a pearl of a bathman. He was a strong, slow, blue-eyed, light-colored Silesian peasant, who had once possessed a scalp full of sandy hair, but had lost at least half of it in his journey to middle life. His whole appearance, and especially his smooth, shining pate, reeked with an indescribably cool, dewy expression, which made one think of cucumbers, wet pebbles, drenched roses, or heads of lettuce after a shower. Neuville insisted that he gained this fresh appearance by living on such things as celery and water-cresses, and by sleeping in one of the cisterns, or perhaps down a well like a bullfrog. It may be, indeed, that the instinct of association deceived us, and that we imputed this aqueous nature to the man solely because he had so much to do with our baths; but, however that was, we certainly never looked at him without being impressed with the idea that he would slice up cold and juicy, like a melon or a tomato.

Franz exhibited a forty-hostler power in rubbing us down, and had, perhaps, curried the hides of our quadruped predecessors in the building. In fact, when I think of his frictions, and consider how wet I was at the time, I almost wonder that I was not rubbed out of existence, like a pencil-mark. Occasionally it was impossible not to shout or stamp under the excitation, at which times the old Russian below would bombard our floor with his boots, in token of disapprobation.

Among so many homely people as we had about us, there were necessarily some whose ugliness ran into eccentricity, if not absurdity. Neuville, who had an extraordinary faculty at discovering resemblances between men and beasts, or birds, soon fixed on one old gentleman as the Owl; and I was obliged to confess that, bating the claws, the said human certainly did bear a striking likeness to the solemn anchorite of ornithology. He was a man of about sixty, with light gray hair, light gray beard, and a light gray suit of clothes, so that, from a distance, you might suppose him to be dressed in light gray feathers. He was tolerably bare of chin, and his mouth had retired under a bower of light gray mustaches. His long, curved nose looked wonderfully like a beak, and his eyes were always wide open with an expression of unqualified astonishment. However early we rose, however fast and far we went, we invariably met him already returning, as if he had started out for his morning walk some time the day previous. Neuville affirmed that he staid in the woods all night, and amused himself with hooting and chasing field-mice until daybreak, when he would leave off at the approach of the earliest patients, and hurry down to the Establishment to take a bath.

Another interesting personage was a middle-aged, muscular Hungarian, with startling black eyes and wavy black beard, who had the fame of being crazy, or at least unreasonably original. He carried an enormous yellow cane, one end of which was fash-

ioned into a passable flute.   He always walked alone,
like a man who had dealings with fairies and wood-
nymphs ; and, when he thought no human being was
within hearing, he would put his cane to his lips, and
treat his elfin friends to a melody.   If a wandering
fellow-patient came upon him in one of these dulcet
moments, he dropped the end of his cane, whisked it
about unconcernedly, and looked all around, or up into
the clouds, as if he wondered who the deuce made those
noises.   I suspected him of being Orpheus, who, it will
be remembered, was in the cold water line, and had a
fancy for playing airs to rocks, fishes, and other dumb
creatures.

They told us at Graefenberg of a Mexican who came
there a year or two before us for the sake of trying the
cure on his dyspepsia.   He went through his first
packing with great indignation, and was then taken
down stairs into that horrible abyss of plunge-baths.
Priessnitz pointed to the cistern and bade him get into
it.   "Never!" he thundered; and, marching up stairs,
he dressed himself, and went straight back to Mexico.
Another man in the same situation is said to have fallen
on his knees before Priessnitz, exclaiming, "Oh sir,
remember that I have a wife and children!"

Directly opposite us at table sat an excellent old
gentleman, a wealthy merchant from Hamburg.   Naturally thin and grizzly, in addition dilapidated like our
whole company, he had a ludicrously astonished way
of looking over his spectacles whenever any one addressed him, if it were only to say "Good-morning."
He seemed to be lost in some chaos far away from
outer life, wandering, perhaps, through the interior

gloom of his own invalidism. At the sound of a voice he raised his head slowly; the round eyes and round spectacles settled upon the speaker, one above another, like the ports of a two-decker about to open fire; and then, collecting his vagrant faculties, he would smile and utter a few words of overflowing grave good-nature. He spoke English pretty well, and, like all Germans, was willing to put his linguistic knowledge in practice on every possible occasion. He took an especial fancy to Burroughs, inviting him, if he went to Hamburg, to visit his family. Indeed, this Georgian comrade of mine, young, gay, full of mirth and conversation, insinuating in manners, had rapidly become a pet among our congress of invalids, and was on terms of intimate companionship with men even between whom and himself there was no bond of common language. I doubt not but many of them still remember him with occasional kindly laughter. For my part, I can not speak of him with sufficient gentleness; for he is already numbered in the sacred company of the dead, a victim to the yellow fever of Savannah.

Next to our Hamburg friend sat a tolerably pretty and intolerably haughty Prussian lady, the wife of some government official, and therefore, according to German etiquette, always addressed by the title of her august husband. She sometimes made use of our grave neighbor as an interpreter between herself and our Georgian; and once she signified, in a jesting way, that when she came to America she should pay him a visit.

"Tell her," replied Burroughs, with Oriental magnificence, "that if she will come and see me I will give her five hundred negroes to wait on her."

C

The old Hamburgher, incapable of suspecting a joke, opened his eyes to an unaccustomed extent at such an extravagance of hospitality. "I think," said he, after a moment's reflection, "that five would be better than five hundred."

He translated the splendid proffer, which was received with a hearty laugh, and went the rounds of the lady's acquaintance with great success. From that time forward, Burroughs's consequence, and, indeed, that of our whole party, was considerably increased in the eyes of the Graefenbergers. A man who could be courteous to the amount of five hundred negro waiters was worth smiling upon.

Several members of our invalid regiment were veterans in point of service. A tall, gray-headed Swedish count, who occupied a little cottage by himself, and cultivated its diminutive garden with his own hands, had been under cure eleven years. A rosy German baron, of about sixty-five, was three years his senior in hydropathic experiences. "I am very well," he used to say in explanation, "very well as long as I stay here; but as soon as I go away I get sick again. The regular doctors can do nothing for me. I have tried them all, and taken every one of their drugs, with no result except spoiling my stomach. Accordingly, every time that I have left Graefenberg I have been obliged to return to it. At last I have resolved to settle here for life. Why not? I have plenty of respectable society. I live at Freiwaldau, where I can have good food and lodging. I am incurable; our honest Priessnitz tells me so himself; but as long as I remain here I do not suffer. Why not remain? Of course."

Still another noticeable hydropath was a bald, fat-headed, capacious Parisian, of about forty, round as a puncheon, and very similar to one in other respects. In plain words, he was an occasional drunkard, who had been coaxed to Graefenberg by his friends in a hope that the cure might rid him of his unfortunate appetite. Priessnitz had done his utmost in the way of cold water and warm expostulations; had even ordered the hotel-keepers of Freiwaldau, under penalty of his very powerful displeasure, not to furnish Monsieur Cognac with any spirituous drinks; but all to no purpose. By all sorts of invisible ways and underground railroads, the forbidden thing would find its passage to the unfortunate man's stomach and brain. As he held a respectable position in society and visited nice people, he sometimes produced considerable scandal by the contrast between his conduct and his company. During one of his staggery moments he happened in on a nervous American lady, and quite alarmed her by what she considered his eccentric behavior. The next day he came again, full of dim, regretful recollections, and voluble with apologetical explanations. He had had a crisis, he said—some kind of nervous crisis—in fact, he had such turns frequently; they were the symptoms of his peculiar malady. He hoped he had said nothing disagreeable to Madame; sometimes his attacks were so violent that he hardly knew what he said; he prayed that she would excuse him, and believe that he was her most respectful though unworthy servant.

There was a tall, stout grenadier of a Swedish count, in the prime of life, who was also one of our notables.

He nursed a curious fancy of stealing away into the woods, dressed in nothing at all, not even a collar, and strolling about thus attired, with an axe in his hand, to the great confusion, doubtless, of all the undines and tree-nymphs. His idea was to take a copious air-bath, warming himself at intervals by a few chops at wayside saplings; and he thought that these occasional returns to a primitive state of existence had a most invigorating effect on his physical and moral nature. He used to manage his sylvan escapades from the douche-houses, wretched little huts well retired within the leafy solitude of the forest. "Oh, not at all," said he, in answer to some one who asked him if such promenades *à la* garden of Eden did not sometimes lead him into embarrassing situations. "I meet no one but strawberry-girls, and they only laugh and get out of my way."

The prettiest of all our patients—the only beautiful one, I verily believe, among them—was a little baroness of eighteen or nineteen summers, from Vienna. With a clear brunette complexion flushing on the cheek into roses, the brightest of black eyes, features sufficiently regular, and a plump but graceful form, she would have been attractive in any place, or amid any constellation of fair women; but, floating through our medley of varied ugliness, she was delightful. I never saw her without her mother, who, like all Continental mammas, held that maidenhood demands the watchfulness of little less than giants and dragons. My nearest intimacy with her, unfortunately, or perhaps fortunately, was to know several of her acquaintance. One of them, an American, told me that she was a fresh and simple child of nature; another, a French count, laughed at the idea, and affirmed that she was a coquette. I incline to the opinion of the Frenchman; firstly, because I think he was the best judge of European manners; secondly, because I imagine my countryman to have been a little in love with the *petite baronne*.

This pretty girl came to Graefenberg, a few months before my arrival, so deadly sick with a heart disease that no one thought she could live. Priessnitz refused to undertake her cure, saying that she was too far gone for any hope, and would probably die under the first baths; but, at the earnest entreaties of her relatives, he revoked his decision and commenced her treatment, washing his hands, however, of all responsibility. At the first envelopment in the wet sheet, her heart beat so violently that its pulsations were distinctly visible through the usual covering of three blankets. She survived this opening struggle, and thenceforward convalesced rapidly. When I saw her she used to climb the steep hills around Graefenberg with such an aspect of health as if she had never been ill, nor would be so forever.

CHAPTER VII.

GRAEFENBERGESSES AND GRAEFENBERGIANISMS.

I OUGHT to say one word of the native beauties of Graefenberg. When I speak of them as beauties, it makes me laugh to think how ugly they were; but I ought to be ashamed of myself, for it was no laughing matter to the poor creatures themselves. As there were a number of wealthy families in the borough of Freiwaldau, there were, of course, some young ladies there who dressed well, and considered themselves aristocratic. But, however genteel, they were not handsome, and had, in particular, a dropsical, cadaverous look, as if overbleached in their papas' linen-factories. I never tried to talk to them; common sense forbade it; I spoke no German.

The only damsels of the locality with whom it was easy to come to an understanding were the peasant girls, who collected every morning around the House fountain to sell us cakes, strawberries, and cherries. Jovial, laughing bodies all of them, several were rather pretty in a coarse way, by reason of merry blue eyes, mouths full of fine teeth, and cheeks full of dimples. One of them, who did me the favor of officiating as my washer-woman, was really handsome, as far as regular features, a clear rosy skin, a small coral mouth, and a nicely-rounded form are sufficient to constitute handsomeness. The advantages of shoes were acknowledged by these nymphs; but they scorned stockings, and wore economical frocks reaching only six inches below the knee, in consequence of which they made a startling display of solid sun-burnt legs, generally well modeled, and not seldom profusely scratched by the thickets and brambles through which they waded to collect their horticultural merchandise. Alas for the romance of these sylvan scenes! these daughters of nature were decidedly more frail than fair, the morals of the peasantry for miles around Graefenberg having been lamentably corrupted by its unscrupulous bachelor patients. Much evil, Priessnitz said, had been brought into the district by his establishment, and no good thing besides money.

As for the young ladies of our invalid set, and old ladies too, I had a fair opportunity of seeing them at their best, in the balls which took place twice a week in the great dining-hall. On Sunday evenings and Thursday evenings the chairs and tables were huddled into one end of the room, so as to give space to dancing and flirtation. Directly over the principal door a small gallery trembled under a riotous mob of fiddles and trumpets, which some laborious Silesian peasants vainly tried to reduce to melodious order. The society was as mixed a one as could easily be collected in the Hartz Mountains of a Walpurgis night, all languages, classes, and manners being there represented, from Americans to Russians, and from dukes to dog-doctors.

As Priessnitz insisted that every one should dance who could, it naturally happened that some people tried to dance who could not. I remember one unlucky individual, apparently troubled with the string-halt, who twitched his legs after him in a style that was too much for the gravity of us youth, and who, as he made the circle of the saloon in a waltz or polka, was followed by an epidemic smile shooting from face to face, as if he were some planet of mirthfulness, dispensing a splendor of broad grins upon every thing which bordered his orbit. Then there was an indiscreet little man in black, who invariably coupled himself with the tallest woman present, and manœuvred her about the hall with the helpless jerkings of a jolly-boat trying to tow a frigate. Many of the guests, however, showed themselves natural and experienced dancers, managing their heels with an eloquence of motion which put to shame the inarticulate bleating of the wretched music.

The favorite dance was a wild gallop, much like a steeple-chase in point of reckless rapidity, whirling people around the enchanted circle with the briskness and rumpled confusion of hens blown about like a whirlwind. A very advantageous step it was for those ladies who had pretty ankles; and for this artistic reason it was as popular with the outsiders as with the performers. But the finest thing of all was a thundering Polish mazurka, emphasized with heavy boots, in a style which made one feel as if he were enveloped in a charge of cavalry.

The balls usually commenced at half past seven, and continued vehemently until half past nine, when the patients began to drop off to their chambers. Priessnitz was almost always present, attended by his family, a pleasant smile playing on his red-oak face, while he talked with the old fellows who had the honor of his intimacy, or gazed approvingly at the higgledy-piggledy whirl of feet and faces. Here, as every where, he spoke little, and I presume that he had few ideas except such as were good to put in practice; for I understood that he had never learned to read until he was twenty-five, and that even now his lections were limited to an occasional newspaper. Near him usually sat Mrs. Priessnitz, a rather hard-featured, careful-eyed woman, not as kindly in manner as her husband, and, to all appearance, still more taciturn. The eldest daughter I never saw, thanks to an attractive dowry by which she had secured a Hungarian noble for her husband. The second daughter, a pale and rather haughty blonde of eighteen, neither handsome nor homely, was one of the best and most frenetic of the dancers. When nine o'clock came, the old couple quietly walked off, leaving their absence as a hint to the revelers that it was time to wet their bandages and go to bed.

Among such a number of young gallants and people made irritable by indigestions, gouts, and neuralgias, it was natural that insults should sometimes be passed which nothing but blood and gunpowder could expiate. A very interesting squabble took place on the occasion of an associated ball, given by ten or a dozen leading dandies (or *lions*, as they say in French) of our savage society. One of the managers was a corpulent Frenchman, named D'Hauteville, a social, civil man, like most of his countrymen, as long as he was well treated, but sufficiently quick on the trigger for all fighting purposes. Among the invited was a

long, awkward, tow-headed Austrian lieutenant, a Saxon by birth, quite a young fellow, but so insufferably
conceited that you wanted to quarrel with him at first
sight.   To prevent confusion in the supper-room, it
had been agreed that the managers alone should hand
refreshments to the ladies.   Our Saxon, despising this
sumptuary law and its enactors, escorted a couple of
damsels to the tables, and proceeded to furnish them
liberally with whatever he could lay his sprawling
hands on.   D'Hauteville softly remonstrated in his
long ears, repeating the above-mentioned agreement,
and begging him to submit to some little unavoidable
delay rather than open a scene of confusion.   The lieutenant replied that his ladies had already waited an
annoying time for hungry people, who doubtless wore
wet bandages, and that he should now see to it himself that they received the proper convivial attentions.
D'Hauteville retorted, with the spunk of the true Gal-
lic cock, that he should prevent him ; and in a moment
both parties were ready to disembowel each other with
their dessert-spoons, a species of contest in which the
Frenchman would have been at a great disadvantage by
reason of his superior abdominal development.   They
were separated for the moment, however, and the evening passed off without further disturbance.

    The next day, every body concerned wanted satis-
faction, and the result was a resolution to settle the
matter by pistols and surgeons.   A rendezvous of
death was appointed in Prussia, some eight or ten
miles from Graefenberg, and a couple of sorry hacks
bore to it the proposed combatants, with their train of
Job's comforters.   On the way, in consequence of the

badness of the roads or the horses, the lieutenant had so much time for reflection, and employed it also to so amiable a purpose, that he resolved, before he would fight, to see all the laws of honor where they came from, that is, in Tophet. Arrived at the ground, he made the explanations that he would not make ten hours before, retracted all his offensive remarks, and, in consequence, spoiled the fun of the seconds. They were as indignant as disappointed people usually are, especially those who are called out of bed for nothing; and they subsequently treated the placable young man's feelings with great inhumanity, insisting that he should resign his commission.

Another duel actually came off between an Austrian officer, whose name I have forgotten, and an English lieutenant called Drummond. The Austrian, having taken a great fancy to Drummond, improved every opportunity of seizing him by the button-hole and inflicting upon him certain lengthened conversations. His love was but ill requited, for Drummond considered him a bore from the first, and liked him all the less as they became more intimate. Such a contrariety of pulling on the cords of friendship could not last long without producing a rupture; and Drummond, who was nervous by right of dyspepsia, soon grew excessively irritable under the Austrian's familiarities, like a snappish dog who gets indignant at little Bobby's affectionate but awkward attachment to his tail.

Happening to meet one morning when the wind was due east, the Austrian bowed as usual, but his over-wearied friend passed on without vouchsafing a look in reply.   The forsaken one halted with a martial stare of indignant wonder ; but, remembering that Englishmen are eccentric, he resolved to wait for further developments before he considered himself insulted.   A short time afterward they encountered again, and the Austrian repeated his salute.   Drummond turned his back on him, and marched off with a gesture of supreme contempt.   The next morning he received a call from a friend of his late friend, who, after a ceremonious bow, made known that his business was to demand explanation of certain irreverent conduct of Lieutenant Drummond toward Captain Whatshisname-stein of the Austrian army.

"Certainly," said Drummond.   "The truth is, that I am tired of your friend's acquaintance, and want to relieve myself of it.   I did my best, in a civil way, to make him understand that he bored me.   He would not take a hint, and I had to insult him.   That is the whole affair."

"Of course, then, you are ready to grant him the only satisfaction that remains to a gentleman in his cirumstances ?"

"Of course.   All he wants—whenever he pleases."

"My principal, being the injured party, has a right to the choice of arms.   Still, he desires to know whether there is any particular weapon that you would prefer."

"No ; any thing—any thing that he likes."

"Are you acquainted with the use of the broadsword ?"

"Not at all."

"I am sorry.   It is the weapon of predilection in

the Austrian service for such occasions, and the one which my principal would choose before all others."

"Oh, don't hesitate on my account. Let it be the broadsword, if your friend at all desires it; and the broader the better."

Accordingly, broadsword it was, the next morning, in a high-pitched room in one of the hotels of Freiwaldau.

Drummond had time to take a lesson or two in sabre exercise from the fencing-master of the village, so as not to be delivered up to his adversary's blade unresistingly. Fencing lessons, in such pressing cases, always consist of a few simple parries, with two or three only of the most prudent offensive strokes. The novice is strongly counseled to stand as much as possible on guard, and to make very cautious cuts at his *vis-à-vis*, reserving even these until the chance is palpable. As German duels usually end with the first blood drawn, this method of fighting is very favorable to green hands ; and the skirmish generally closes with some insignificant scratch, which does not always fall upon the least practiced of the combatants.

Drummond followed out this system of tactics with great coolness and success. Parrying carefully the wrathful storm of blows which fell on his sabre, he at last got a chance to let in a hit of his own, grazing his opponent's arm, and sending a small streak of crimson down the bare white skin. Observing the blood, and supposing that satisfaction had been given, he neglected to recover guard, and received a light tap on the shoulder from the German, who, it seems, was unconscious of being wounded. Drummond brought up his

sabre again, and administered another mild slash ; for
his opponent had, in turn, dropped guard at sight of
the bloody shoulder.   All this passed like lightning,
and before the seconds could interfere to prevent the
double mistake, which certainly appears in a most comical light if the reader will only consider that a couple
of heads might have been whipped off by it.   It will be
observed, also, that the confident, experienced swordsman had received two wounds, and the cautious novice
only one.   The duel was now over, and honor satisfied ; nothing remained but to settle the disagreement.
The seconds called on the principals to shake hands
and forget their differences.

"I will shake hands," said Drummond, "but not
forget the difference.   It is unreasonable to expect me
to take all this trouble to get rid of a man's acquaintance, and then continue as intimate with him as before.   Here is my hand, but on condition that we keep
apart hereafter."

The Germans agreed to this proposition out of respect to English eccentricity, and Drummond left the
room, charmed at having got quietly rid of his troublesome admirer.   I ought to add that I witnessed neither of these affairs, and, therefore, relate their history
at second-hand, which is as safe a hand as a man can
have in a duel.

CHAPTER VIII.

THE CURES OF GRAEFENBERG.

WHETHER the Silesians are naturally given to heterodox methods of doctoring, or whether simply the success of Priessnitz had generated imitators, I can not decide; but one or other of these causes had favored the neighborhood of Graefenberg with a variety of odd establishments for the healing of diseases. There was a *Curd Cure*, wherein sick people were fed exclusively on curdled milk, and, if I was rightly informed, put asoak in it. There was a *Straw Cure*, wherein the patients not only drank intemperately of straw tea, but were horribly tormented by being put naked inside of straw beds, and kept there until they were nearly flayed by the points and edges of this medicinal fodder. And, about two miles from Graefenberg, in the valley of the little stream of Freiwaldau, was still another eccentric hospital devoted to a method of treatment called the *Wine Cure*. Here horrible sweatings, of eight hours, in numerous dry blankets, made the nights miserable; while a curious system of diet, arranged on a sliding scale, carried the patients through all the stages of starvation and repletion, commencing with abundant meals, and descending gradually to the circumscribed rations of three small rolls a day; then creeping up the digestive staircase again to aldermanic breakfasts and dinners, and so on, up and down, until the sufferer was either cured, buried, or driven to the desperation of flight. In compensation for this sharp mortification of the flesh, a considerable daily portion of wine was allowed, and on Saturdays double treats. D'Hauteville told me that, happening in there one Saturday afternoon, he found the patients and the doctor all fuddled together. One old acquaintance, too glad to see him to wait till he could reach the door, stuck his fist through a pane of glass to shake hands, after which he hallooed riotously, declaring that he felt better every minute, and denouncing Priessnitz as a quack and cold water as a nuisance.

Singular as it may seem, this system often effected cures, and drew over various renegades from Graefenberg. One of these apostates from cold water told me that he and his comrades suffered very little from hunger during the long fasts above mentioned, and seemed to lose their appetites in proportion as their food was diminished. Still, the wine-doctor's severe sweatings and dietings were exceedingly hard upon delicate constitutions, and, on the whole, his practice, like that of a Kentucky rifleman, was apt to be attended by very sudden deaths. Personally he was a tall, heavy, hulking fellow of about fifty, with the tone and manners of an unmistakable peasant. He pretended to be the predecessor of Priessnitz in medicine ; he was even profane enough to tell us that the great Graefenberger was only his imitator.

As for our party in the stable, we remained faithful to cold water, unseduced by the fascinations of curds, straw tea, or even wine cures. We took four baths a day, at a minimum, and occasionally more. In opposition to a light fever, Neuville once accomplished fifteen packings between sunrise and bedtime. However violent an illness might be, people at Graefenberg never betook themselves to their beds, but rather to supplementary waterings and walkings. I knew an English lady, the wife of a Swiss clergyman, who, to drive off an inflammation of the lungs, was dashed with handfuls of cold water for a couple of hours together; and, when she was so completely chilled that no surface heat remained any where, except a little about her head, a couple of stout bathwomen took her by the arms and walked her to and fro until the circulation returned. Two operations of this sort, followed by a sound night's sleep, expelled, or, in the words of Priessnitz, *froze out* the inflammation.

A young Dantzicker, who had been pestered for three months by an intermittent fever, was stripped, folded in a dripping wet sheet, and seated by an open window through which a strong draught was flowing. From time to time, as his envelopment gave signs of drying, he was doused with a pailful of water. Two hours of this treatment scattered the fever for three days, and, when it reappeared, a second session of the same nature so disgusted it, that, like an exorcised devil, it decamped and returned no more.

Such cases as these, however, were extreme ones, and our good doctor was sometimes cautious to an appearance of timidity. A stout, florid Italian lady, bearing semblance of unvaried health, told me that Priessnitz refused to give her any of the usual baths, and would submit her to no operation beyond a slight rubbing with dampened towels. She begged hard to be allowed the wet sheet, which is also a moist rubbing, but of a much moister quality.   Priessnitz consented unwillingly, and told the bathwoman to send for him in case of any alarming result.   The wet sheet was applied, and brought on an immediate fit of violent hysterics—an excellent proof, I thought, of the peasant-doctor's prudence and keen professional insight.

One case which I witnessed excited a great deal of admiration among the patients, as it was one of the marvelous cures which sometimes happened at Graefenberg.   A pleasant-faced Hungarian girl came to the Establishment, with one eye totally blinded, and the sight of the other failing.   Every day I saw her pass and repass our rooms, her head swathed with wet bandages, her steps guided by the arm of an elder sister.   After two or three weeks of the treatment, the light went away altogether from her dark orbs, and she was completely sightless.   People muttered loudly at the poor girl's misfortune, and attributed it to the rashness or clumsiness of the doctor.   Priessnitz said that the visual nerve had been paralyzed by an internal ulcer, which would soon break, and give way to a rapid recovery.   Great was the wonder of Graefenberg at the result; for at the end of a week or so this hazardous prophecy became fact : a discharge of matter took place, and both the girl's eyes resumed their vision.

The effect of the cure on myself was not such in manner as I had anticipated, but was, if any thing, more than I had presumed to hope.   Some years of unrewarded obedience to doctors and of fruitless foragings in apothecaries' shops had taught me to put little trust in great medicines of whatsoever description.

Still, there was a fascination in the labors of hydropathy, an epidemic in the immense faith of every one around me, which made me look forward with vague expectation to quick and satisfactory results. I waited for a crisis of some strange sort—a fever, an eruption, or as many boils as Job, and then a sudden falling of the burden from my weary shoulders. What I found was a gradual increase of strength, a hitherto unknown power of enduring fatigue, a new buoyancy of hope and cheerfulness. Day by day the spirit of my dream changed from sickness to health, until I discovered to my surprise that I was recovering without a miracle. I learned to walk ten miles over the hills in the early morning without other stomachic support than water, and felt after it, when I sat down to breakfast, as if I could eat not only the sour milk before me, but the cow that gave it. There was no fatigue from which a bath would not raise me, and send me out again to track the mountain paths until my long-tasked muscles demanded another invigoration from the benevolent water-naiad. To the habitual invalid, to him who feels it for the first time in years, or perhaps in life, there is no sensation more glorious, more superhuman, than the consciousness of abounding and sufficient strength. All labors seem so easy, all trials so insignificant, all nature so friendly and sympathizing.

Yet, notwithstanding all the benefits received at Graefenberg, I left it before my cure was half completed. The climate, as I have said, was detestable. It rained nearly half the time, even when it was fair weather. The winds were as cold as if they slept in wet sheets, and blew all the while, without pause or

punctuation.   The food was an insult to the palate
and an injury to the stomach.   I knew not the difference in hydropathic physicians, and hoped to find, in
some more supportable locality, another as skillful as
Priessnitz.   D'Hauteville told me of places in his
country where I could continue my cure, and, at the
same time, practice good French instead of bad German.   Thus, after a residence of two months at Graefenberg, I wandered away in the company of Burroughs,
and, now seeking a ruined castle, now a water-cure,
traversed middle Germany with all the haunted Rhine-
land.

CHAPTER IX.

DIVONNE, OR MERMANHOOD IN FRANCE.

OUR obliging secretary of legation at Paris, Mr. Henry Sandford, interested himself in the object of my search, and soon discovered the locality and circumstances that I wanted. In the southeastern part of France, said he, fifteen minutes' walk from the Swiss frontier, and one hour's walk from Lake Leman, you will find the new and highly-recommended hydropathic establishment of Divonne.

I left Paris in the Genevan diligence, and amused myself for about forty hours in looking out of the *coupé* windows. I observed that the hills were too rounded and bare of trees, the meadow lands too few, and the vineyards too much like bean-fields, to permit any great number of charming landscapes. I was vexed to see that the picturesque old chateaux with pointed towers had been mostly pulled down and replaced by whitewashed boxes of the renaissance order, dating chiefly, I thought, from the tasteless times of Louis XV. I judged from the faces and manners of the French peasantry that they were own cousins to the Irish peasantry, particularly when I came upon a quartet of them dancing gayly in wooden shoes, on a muddy road, of a rainy day. I was reminded of Puss-in-boots when I saw the postillions up to their waists in ponderous cowhide; and I turned from their absurd bobtailed coats to a recollection of those elders of Is-

rael who had their skirts cut off about their middles by
Hanun, king of the Ammonites.   The reader stares,
perhaps, and wonders whether this is all that I saw in
passing through France the beautiful.   I reply that I
saw many other things, but that he has already heard
of them, even to greater satiety than of these.

At Dijon the coupé received two other travelers,
brothers, by birth Scotchmen, by residence Londoners.
At first they took me for an aborigine, and one of them
made in rheumatic French some advances toward an
intimacy.   Our conversation hobbled in a helpless
style until each saw plainly that the other was no
Gaul, and then, with a bound of delighted surprise,
it sailed airily away on its native wings of English.

From the top of the brown Jura we descended by a
sinuous road into an astonishing valley, where Lake
Leman shone splendidly in a setting of mountains,
while to the south, under the bridges of Geneva, flowed away the humid glitter of the Rhone, and behind
towered, in blinding whiteness, the sublime brotherhood of Swiss mountains.   Furiously down the zig-
zag descent rattled the diligence, grating dangerously
around sharp corners, and exposing, in rapid succession, now one side and now the other to the vast under landscape.   As it tacked and veered, our three
wondering faces clustered alternately on the right-hand
or left-hand window, peeping out like inquisitive young
opossums from the omnibus of their mother's corpo-
rality.

"You don't mean to say that those are the real
Alps?" said the younger Scotchman, pointing with the
stem of his clay pipe at Mont Blanc and Company.

"To be sure they are," responded his brother, who had seen them before.

"Dear me! God bless me! how remarkably small they are! Why, I expected to see them stick up right over my head. Where's the tobacco, Jim? I'll take another smoke."

"For shame, you barbarian! Talk about smoking when there is such scenery to be looked at!"

"Have patience, Jim. I shall grow up to the sentiment by-and-by, I suppose, but they look confounded small at present." And here the disappointed sightseer curled himself back in the middle of the coupé to puff at the consolatory Virginia. How many a man has experienced this same dwarfing of emotion when he has at last come in sight of the Alps, Niagara, Rome, Raphael, or any other bourne of gigantic expectation!

At the *Hotel de la Couronne* I summoned the head waiter, and inquired what he knew of Doctor Vidart's hydropathic conveniences and capacities. " Sir," he replied, " I am acquainted well with the place. I have not myself visited it, but Madame, the proprietress of this hotel, was there cured of a malady. Let me assure you, sir, that you will there be very content; you will there find a doctor of much capacity and a society very agreeable."

Thus encouraged, I took coach the next day for Divonne. Over the translucent Rhone, right by the green, breezy island of Rousseau, along the ineffable beauty of Lake Leman, through a country of neat cottages and costly villas, a couple of sorry horses bore me in two hours to the gates of Doctor Paul Vidart, where I descended, and made application for a hospitable admittance. Yes, there was a chamber at the service of Monsieur; yes, Monsieur the Doctor was with himself; yes, the porter should cause the baggages to mount immediately ; yes, said the gay Savoyard portress to all my questions and all my demands.

Lodgings secured, face and hands washed, I received a visit from the doctor, a handsome, portly man of thirty-five, with something of the dignity of his retired surgeonship from the French army, and all the jovial, easy politeness which is the birthright of most Frenchmen. My performance of the salutations was tolerable, but I found it a far harder thing to describe symptoms and understand prescriptions, and I tried to evade the difficulty. Alas! he had no knowledge of English; he regretted that he could boast no speaking acquaintance with the Italian; he knew a little Arabic, which was entirely at my service if agreeable, but his language was French.

Courage, perseverance, and a pocket dictionary carried me victoriously through the trial. The doctor and I came to an understanding, which, I am happy to say, was never followed by a misunderstanding. Speaking of pocket dictionaries, by the way, I may as well confess that I used my *dictionnaire de poche* for some months before I discovered that *Poche* was not the author of it.

The doctor gone, I wandered down stairs, and strolled about the grounds of the establishment. Young trees waved over neat flower-bands and graveled walks, while here a swan-fountain poured forth its cool luxury, and there a small jet flung up its trembling pillar of spray. The buildings were three in number : a long stone affair, originally a factory; a modern addition, containing the saloon, dining-hall, and kitchen; finally, in separate dignity, behind a large oak, the small but comfortable house of the doctor. A roofed passage, which was really a bridge, spanning a swift rivulet of the purest, gayest water, united the two edifices of the establishment proper.

The patients had apparently sought shelter indoors from the monotonous drizzle of an autumnal rain, and no one was about besides myself and a shaggy, undersized dog, who had taken up a position on three legs beneath the oak-tree. He seemed to be a humorist, for, as I passed him, he put his tongue in his cheek, or, rather, out of one corner of his mouth, and eyed me with a quizzical expression, which seemed to say, "There's another of 'em; you'll see him in the brook to-morrow. I know where they'll put him; it isn't a warm, dry place neither."

The saloon was a ground-floor room, thirty or thirty-five feet long, simply furnished, though gorgeous now to my mind's eye with all the gay hours that I afterward spent there. I noticed pillars to sustain the ceiling, crimson curtains over the tall windows, a piano near the fireplace, and modern French novels strewed about the tables. As the hour-hand of a mantel-clock verged toward one, hungry patients filed in to the number of three or four dozen, and presently a short, stupid waiter (who twice afterward basted my coat with gravy) invited us, in horrible Alsatian French, to enter the dining-hall. Sailing in quietly and decently, we halted with our faces to a long table, like a shoal of well-behaved fishes with their noses to the bait.

D

Being the last comer, I was seated very near the lower end, between a short, yellow-headed Swiss, and a tall, black-headed Frenchman.   The dinner was excellent, and I felt that I was in a civilized country, where I need have no fears, as at Graefenberg, lest the next dish should be boiled gentleman and lady.   The knives and forks rattled cheerfully, but not boisterously, and above all rose a courteous mirthfulness of French talk and laughter.

Before reaching Divonne I had made the resolution to speak French there, or perish in the attempt.   I commenced on my yellow-haired comrade, who seemed glad of the provocation, and bombarded me for the space of an hour with a whole arsenal of unintelligible questions and observations.   However, I bore up gallantly under the assault, guessed out some of his meanings, made him comprehend several of mine, and felt, on the whole, heroic, confident, victorious.   Now and then I glanced up the line of guests to get an idea of the character and appetites of my present associates. At the head appeared the portly figure, regular features, and merry eye of the doctor, his lips parting at every moment to let in a morsel or let out a sentence, while now and then the gleam of his small white teeth prefaced a shout of laughter, the echo of some good joke or comic story.   On his left sat his brother, remarkable for the same broad frame, blue eye, and Grecian nose, but graver, more reposeful, and more taciturn. Beside the two were their wives, small, quiet Swiss ladies, almost eclipsed, both physically and morally, by the robustious presence of their husbands.   A chair or two below the doctor sat a dark-browed man of middle age, who was pointed out to me as Frederick Monod, one of the most distinguished Protestant ministers in France, an embodiment of no sanctimonious misanthropy, but rather of a genial sympathy with humanity, in its happiness as well as in its misery. He and the doctor seemed to keep up a perpetual popping of gay repartees, like two baskets of Champagne bombarding each other with alternate mirthful corks and hilarious foam-spouts. Below them several decorous ladies and bright *demoiselles* listened earnestly over their plates, echoing back the jokes with frequent laughter. One girl of fifteen attracted my attention by a remarkably handsome face—one of the prettiest, in fact, that I had yet seen in Europe. Very beautiful hazel eyes, regular features, and a rich brunette color, with an expression strangely mingled of reserve and cleverness, made a whole that shines distinctly yet in my memory. Like all good French girls in the presence of their mothers or of strangers, she had a timid air, and seldom gave utterance to her little fancies.

Below Ida came a long row of comparatively uninteresting jaws, some feminine, some bearded, but all hard at work over their food or their conversation. Two or three conscious button-holes blushed with the red ribbon of the Legion of Honor. One gentleman thus adorned had the air of an extremely stupid man, remarkable for nothing but a squint of horrible perverseness. I cautiously inquired of a young Piedmontese, who spoke some English, whether this unpromising legionary had been decorated for strabismus, and my question was politely taken as a very good hit at the facility with which medals and ribbons had been conferred in France. It struck me as possible, also, that the gentleman got his squint subsequently to his embellishment, in consequence of trying to keep one admiring eye always fixed on his honorable button-hole.

The dinner, as I have said, was excellent, simple in its selection of dishes, well cooked, and only faulty in finishing with a dessert of pastry. The doctor afterward confided to me that he suffered this dyspeptic dish out of respect for his numerous Genevese patients, who were nonsensically attached to their preserves and pie-crust. Dinner over, the bachelors and the husbands of bachelor habits (numerous classes both on the Continent) dropped away to the billiard-room, to smoke or to punch the heads of those much-persecuted ivory bullets. The others, deterred from lounging out of doors by the interminable rain, scattered about the spacious parlor. A tall, fair, silent girl from Geneva, a niece of the doctor's wife, sat down to the piano, and played, with admirable execution, a series of waltzes and opera airs. Some listened to the music, some fumbled the illustrated novels and magazines on the table, some kept up the murmur of conversation which had commenced over the soup. As an hour passed on, people dropped away to their rooms, or braved the rain in the peripatetic philosophy of thick boots and umbrellas. There was no insanity here in the cure, no summer cloth for winter weather, no wet toweling for hatless heads, no ostentatious display of bare feet and ankles. Fanaticized as I was by the savage enthusiasm of Graefenberg, I secretly mourned over this effeminacy, fearing lest Divonne should be the Capua of my hydropathic hardihood; and I only waited a better acquaintance with the doctor, or rather with his language, to instill into him more ferocious ideas of the treatment, and a more orthodox zeal for making his patients wholesomely uncomfortable.

At four o'clock, the hour of afternoon immersion, I looked up my particular bathman, and placed myself at his discretion. I was soon hermetically kerneled in a dripping sheet and a stout packing of blankets, the whole being tucked in with a puffy upper crust of feather bed. This last affair was one of those light, downy syllabubs used by the Germans as coverlets, but so insupportably warm as to give one an extravagant idea of the winter comforts of geese, hens, and other feathered creatures. The reaction was rapid under these sultry circumstances, and if I had been an egg, I should certainly have been hatched in fifteen or twenty minutes. In the style of getting down stairs there was a vast improvement upon Graefenberg. Instead of being walked down like a galvanized mummy, I was picked up by two stalwart Swiss and borne off in state, as if I were the Grand Lama or the successful candidate of an Irish election. Deposited on a bench in the clean, spacious bathing-room, I was delighted by finding every desirable luxury in the way of douches, sitting-baths, squirt-guns of various descriptions, plunges, and so forth. Into the great cistern where I was finally emptied there rushed, with a fall of four or five feet, a really respectable rivulet, uproarious, bubbly, translucent, and of an unchanging frigidity throughout the whole round of seasons. This streamlet, the same that once urged the wheels of the mill, took its rise, a quarter of a mile distant, in a magnificent natural spring, which doubtless drew its sparkling treasures through cavernous reservoirs from the snows of the neighboring Jura.

François, my present overseer, was a muscular Swiss, with a moist blue eye, a skin well burned by sunshine and wine, and a nose inclining to scarlet fever at the apex. A soured temper and a muddled intellect completed his resemblance to our old-fashioned cider-guzzlers of New Jersey and New England. Unlike my old Franz of Graefenberg, he was an infidel as regarded the virtues of water, and took no further interest in his profession than to drink something strong in order to keep out the wet. He would never, like Prince Hal, have wasted any astonishment on Falstaff's twopennyworth of bread to an intolerable deal of sack. When I told him of the *Wine-cure*, he was ravished with the idea, and marveled greatly that so excellent a system had not spread over the universe. I one day tried to enforce upon him the impression that it was a sinful inconsistency in him to drink wine while he administered so much water to other people.

"What!" said he, interrupting his scrubbing, and putting his hands on his hips with an air of solemn remonstrance, "we bathmen not drink wine! I should like to know how we would carry all you heavy gentlemen about the house, then. No, no; we poor devils never could do that on water."

François had been a soldier in the service of Holland, and used to entertain me with indistinct accounts of his adventures in that horizontal country. In return, I told him, as well as my ignorance of French would allow, short stories about our Indians and negroes; and, judging from his expressions of astonishment, I flattered myself that I enlarged his information materially concerning the colored and semi-colored races. But, in spite of his advantages, François continued a blockhead, and was at last turned away for getting drunk, beating his wife, and being saucy to the doctor.

At six o'clock there was a heavy supper; another bad idea of our medicine-man. The table exhibited a phalanx of hot meats, cold meats, boiled potatoes, cold milk, scalded milk, but no sour milk. I observed one dyspeptic female lay in two courses of beefsteak for nocturnal digestion, and concluded that she calculated to work them off by taking a ride of nine or ten hours on the nightmare. After supper came another long sitting in the parlor, enlivened by music, reading, sewing, and plenty of conversation, in which last, by the way, I took no part, because I could not speak French, and would not speak English. Before three days had passed, however, I put bashfulness behind me, as I would Satan, and made myself conspicuous by talking incessantly a singular jargon approaching in sound to French. I began sentences without knowing whether I could finish them; held long colloquies of which I scarcely understood my own half; saluted the ladies freely after the sociable Continental fashion; and, in short, made myself perfectly at home in the establishment, to which comfortable end I was greatly aided by the courteous, gregarious nature of my brother and sister invalids.

CHAPTER X.

PASTIMES IN DIVONNE.

A few evenings after my advent in Divonne a quadrille was started, which proved a failure from the lack of capable quadrillians.   Then came something which succeeded better—a series of games after the fashion of "Fox and Geese," or "Button," which, for almost every evening of more than a month, kept us in an uproar of merriment.   Capital players were these French invalids, abounding in queer conceits, rich with perpetual laughter, and as chirrupy as summer birds.   We had all ages and characters in our giggling circle, from grave old Pastor Passevant, with his mild, wrinkled phiz and black velvet cap, down to three flaxen-haired Swedish sisters, none of them yet in their teens.   Now and then, also, a couple of Mr. Monod's sons came over from Geneva ; and being wild-pated, rough-and-tumble urchins, they contributed not a little to the clamorousness of our recreations.

In the game of "Fox and Goose," or, as the French call it, "Cat and Rat," a circle is formed, two deep, around which there is abundance of steeple-chasing, the cat seeking to overtake, and the rat to escape by placing himself inside of one of the couples.   It would have made Timon the Athenian laugh to see our capacious doctor cantering around the ring, hard on the flight of little Marie, the youngest daughter of the Swedish captain, and to hear our general shriek of delight as Marie dodged through some opening in the circle and found a goal of safety. Then, perhaps, Mr. Monod was started out as the fugitive, and away rolled the two big men in a ponderous scamper around the excited spectators. Then it was the turn of Caprini, the slatternly, slipshod Italian, who drew forth new bursts of merriment by the agitated shuffle of his insecure slippers. Then I was the Rat, with the incessant Cat at my flying heels, while plaudits of laughter complimented the vigorous manner in which Young America managed his somewhat extensive traveling apparatus.

After the Cat and Rat had worn themselves completely out, another play came into general favor. I despair of doing it justice, for I doubt whether it is known in America, and no one who has not seen it can form an idea of its risible character. The company formed in a circle facing inward, with some one —Mr. Monod, for instance—in the centre. At the signal to start, Mr. Monod commenced a ludicrous dance, consisting of a series of short jumps, in the performance of which he advanced across the circle, and halted opposite some one, whom we will suppose to have been little Marie Seeman. Marie began the same step now, though remaining stationary, while Mr. Monod, still in a hopping state, lifted up his voice in a sing-song to these words: "*Bonjour, bonjour, commere Marie; comment se porte compere Vidart!*" ("Good-day, good-day, goodwife Mary; how is goodman Vidart?")

Marie, never ceasing her dance, was bound to reply immediately in the same chanting tone: "*Je n'en*

D 2

sais rien, je n'en sais rien ; je m'en vais voir."   ("I
do not know, I do not know ; I'll go and see.")

This dialogue finished, Mr. Monod hopped into Marie's place and became quiescent, while it was her business to hop across the circle to goodman Vidart, and
send him on an errand of inquiry concerning the health
of some other goodman or goodwife.   And thus the
game went on, until we had jumped and sung ourselves tired, or the time-piece on the mantel warned
us that we had best prepare for the morrow.   Sapless
and uninteresting as all this may seem in description,
it was most ludicrous to see it in execution ; to look
on while two persons of contrasting heights and ages
hopped up and down in face of each other, like two
chickens fighting ; to note their arms dangling absurd-
ly by their sides, their heads balanced stiffly, and their
faces crimsoned with laughter.

Then there were riddles, guessings of proverbs, and
various plays attended by forfeits.   It was once allot-
ted to me as a punishment to dance some ridiculous
dance ; and having, in the leisure of my boyhood, mas-
tered the negro *Juba*, I gave it out with marked emphasis.   It proved a season hit ; it was *comique !
charmant ! tres curieux !*   Not only was I called on
for a repetition night after night, but several persons
wanted to learn the step of me ; and one of the most
fanatical in carrying this point was a severe Swiss
minister, a man of the Boanerges type, with stern
black eyes, and a long black beard of apostolic dignity.   Over and over again did my reverend disciple
carefully watch my feet while I danced the Juba, and
then set himself with solemn perseverance to imitate

the complicated caper. Such a blessing followed his
efforts that he very soon had the step at his fingers'
ends, or rather at his toes' ends ; and day after day 1
used to hear him double-shuffle, or hoe corn and dig
potatoes around the billiard-room and down the passage by way of a reaction after his bath. He told me
that he wanted to amuse his children with the dance,
and I only hope that it diverted them as much as it
diverted their papa.

The gem of our little company, the pet of every
body, male and female, the social luxury necessary to
our full enjoyment, was Ida. When half past nine
of the evening came, and she had to go to her aunt's
room, our circle remained like a ring from which the
diamond has been taken. French girls, and girls in
general on the Continent, are kept under such severe
restraint that they can seldom speak or act out their
real character. Silent, reserved, easily embarrassed,
they follow their mothers like shadows, as inseparable,
as quiet, and almost as little noticed. Ida had more
of this repressed manner than usual, and seemed one
of those persons who learn too early to feel in silence,
either hopeless of sympathy, or shrinking from the
idea of being penetrated and known by another. The
heedless merriment of our games was exactly calculated to tear aside this veil, thrown around her by pre-
cocity or education ; and she never appeared so well,
so true to the pretty artlessness of girlhood, as when
she had to sit down and lean her head against the
wall, because the doctor or Mr. Monod was so funny!

In spite of Ida's reserve, and although we always
conversed in a tongue that was foreign to at least one

of us, I could see that she was more than commonly clever.   She played well, danced as girls of fifteen usually dance, had a good knowledge of German, and no bad one of English.   Her accent in our language was just foreign enough to be as delightful as quaint music.   It was accounted very unlucky for us all when, about six weeks after my arrival, Ida's aunt got well, and they consequently left Divonne.   A coach was driven to the door, and piled with trunks so big that it seemed as if there were two or three coaches standing on top of each other.   Madame Duprez kissed all the married ladies, and shook hands with all the ministers ; Ida threw her arms around a girl friend, and both burst into sobs as their wet cheeks touched ; the driver cracked his whip a dozen times in succession; the shaggy horses gave a spasmodic scramble, as if to see which should be foremost ; and, with the grim steadiness of destiny, the black coach-top slid in between my eyes and a pretty face which had aided to light up some weeks of life in a foreign land.

For six weeks or two months after my arrival, a quarter of an hour was devoted every morning to a religious Protestant service held in some private room. It was attended by a majority of the patients, for we were nearly all Protestants, and boasted quite a body of living divinity in the shape of four Swiss clergymen, one English, and the two celebrated brothers, Frederick and Adolph Monod, of Paris.   A chapter of the Bible, a few quiet observations on the text, a hymn, and a short prayer, all in French, constituted the form of devotion.   On Sunday we sometimes went to a neighboring chapel, belonging to the doctor or his brother, where we listened to a regular service and sermon from a Huguenot preacher. Occasionally, too, we walked over to Crassy, a Swiss frontier village about two miles distant, and sat at the feet of its jocund pastor, the Rev. M. Taillefer, a man more given to making sinners laugh than to converting them.

Many of our people were of the most serious, evangelical class in France and Switzerland—such persons as the French respectfully designate as *dévots*, or contemptuously as *Methodistes*. Those from Geneva were followers of Merle d'Aubigné and Cesar Malan ; those from France, of such men as Frederick and Adolph Monod. Hitherto in Europe I had encountered no characters of this type—no approach, even, to the serious piety and incessant Christianizing zeal of these my present companions. They seemed to me the most charming possible examples of those who are commonly called pious people ; amiable in manners, cheerful in conversation, conscious of the beauty of earth and of their brotherhood with humanity, yet never forgetful of their mystic life, their heavenly calling, the price of their redemption. In short, they combined the existence of this world and the existence of the invisible more easily, gracefully, and lovingly than any class of persons that I had before seen. Yet sometimes this mixture of two modes of sentiment and being was carried to such results, that, to my American eyes, they took the form of a strange inconsistency. I remember one pale Swiss lady, of fragile form and impressible nerves, who was possessed by a singular religious zeal, and who, for instance, did not hesitate one Sunday to supply the lack of a clergyman by reading aloud a chapter in the Bible, and then praying before us all, men as well as women, her husband standing among us.   It was, I think, during the afternoon of that very day that I saw her sitting languidly in the saloon, perusing a volume of the Tauchnitz edition of English authors.   I was curious enough to ask her what book she had, for I felt sure that those Tauchnitz bindings covered no works of devotion. Without the slightest hesitation, she placed in my hands some novel of modern society.   I looked in her face earnestly, but there was not a trace of annoyance there at my inquisitiveness; not a remote consciousness of any contrast between the book and the day.

"Ah! it is a novel," I said.

"Yes; my poor head is so wearied that I must give it some relaxation."

She took the romance again, and went on reading with all the placidity of a quiet conscience.

Some years ago, when the Free Kirk of Scotland made its exodus from the Established Church, a similar movement—in fact, an echo of that one—took place in various countries of the Continent.   In most of them, especially in France, it failed miserably. Frederick Monod, formerly one of the best attended preachers in Paris, saw his congregation diminish to sixty or seventy people, principally chambermaids, while his fifteen thousand francs of salary, a large stipend in France, fell to an indefinitely small sum, which came, as the Arabs say, when God pleased. In Switzerland the result was not wonderfully better, and the free congregations mostly, if not universally, found easy room in insignificant chapels.   A good deal of jealousy and ill-will naturally sprang up between the two churches, the stronger one, as it could not persecute the other physically, rather liking to call it hard names and poke fun at it. The term *Methodiste*, especially, is freely applied to the Independents, and generally rolls out of orthodox lips with an intonation of hearty, contemptuous dislike. The *Methodistes*, by the way, are the best Christians of the two, as far as I am capable of judging.

Pastor Taillefer, of Crassy, was of the Established Church, and held Methodists in particular disrelish. As I have already said, he was a jolly man, who had little disposition to trouble a body about heaven or hell, and whose ideas of pastoral duty fitted him as easy as so many old shoes. One Sunday he gave notice that there would be no preaching after dinner, and then drove into Geneva, a distance of fifteen miles, to see M. Poitevin make an ascension with his famous aeronautic pony. I easily excused Madame Lasalle for reading her novel, but I am inclined to be hard upon Pastor Taillefer, and to affirm that he broke the Sabbath. It is possible, indeed, that he thought Poitevin was going clear up, and that he wished to verify his conceptions of the ascent of Elijah ; but I am very much afraid that he was only actuated by a worldly desire to see a balloon.

I have said nothing about the scenery of Divonne, or the interesting objects in its vicinity. It was in France, as I have already observed, but so hard on the borders of Switzerland that a walk of a quarter of a mile eastward brought you to a little bridge, the other end of which rested on the soil of the mountain republic. It was no mountain here, however, for on every side stretched the valley of Lake Leman. Three miles from Divonne, distinctly visible from the hill back of the village, rolled those waves of wonderful beauty which Byron and Rousseau have made famous. Beyond them were the hills of Savoy; and behind these were mountains on mountains, peeping over each other in increasing altitude and pearliness, until the vista closed in the awful pyramid of Mont Blanc; yes, long rows of snowy mountains, like a Titanic army of spectres, towering from north to south through a hundred miles or more, in an array of terrible, blinding whiteness. The sun threw a glorious mantle upon them as he bade them a nightly adieu, and went away into the golden west. Very wonderful also, and such as I have seen in no other part of earth, were the sunrises that came over them in the winter mornings. While the enormous line of peaks still remained of a deathly, ashy white, all the air above them burned with splendor, raying like a halo, as if the mountains were sanctified, and had put on, not only their robes of spotlessness, but their crowns of glory. It is the sole place where I have yet seen sunrises as lovely, brilliant, and impressive as any sunset. Caprini, in a fit of enthusiasm far beyond his character, said that the clime of his native Italy was beckoning to him from across the Alps.

Three miles from Divonne, going toward the lake, was the family residence of the De Staëls. Six or seven miles farther north, directly upon the shore, was Nyon, a picturesque little city surmounted by a gigantic old chateau. In the principal street stood a bronze statue, of rude antique workmanship, which the people called *Maître Jacques;* a grim-visaged, stiff-kneed fellow, in complete armor, who looked as if he might have been a very ungovernable sort of " Master James" while living, but whose sole, placable business it is now to remind people that the *Canton de Vaud* was once no republic, but divided into feudal estates, and ruled by Savoyard governors. I could learn nothing of who *Maître Jacques* was, or what he had done to be thus commemorated, or what he was *maître* of; only I fancied, from the completeness of his knightly harness, that, if he was the master of any thing in particular, it was of the noble art of self-defense. The mystery attached to " Master James" interested me more, perhaps, than his true story could have done, and I never visited Nyon without passing a few moments in the contemplation of his ugly and solemn physiognomy.

Beyond Nyon, on the lake, lay Vevay, and Clarens, and Chillon, and somewhat behind them, on a lofty hill, rose Lausanne; but the reader knows that it is not the purpose of my book to hash up celebrities. Returning to our little, inconsequential Divonne, I will observe that it became quite interesting when you surveyed it in contrast to the Protestant villages of the *Canton de Vaud.* These last were tidy, solidly built, nicely whitewashed, abounding in bee-hives (that tolerably sure sign of a provident people), and inhabited by broad, burly, vigorous men, evidently one of the sturdiest, wealthiest peasant populations in Europe. No neglected fields were visible here; no musty, tumble-down houses; no rag-tag-and-bobtail population.

Divonne, on the contrary, Catholic Divonne, blessed with the true Church, holy water, the Bishop of Freiburg, and all those orthodox advantages, was as mean, dirty a little village as you shall see marring the beauty of a summer's day. A whole company of soldiers kept it in quietness, and secured its allegiance to Paris. Martial law spread her crimson wings over its muddy streets and shabby rooms; scores of bayonets occasionally turned up its asparagus-beds and potato-patches to search for illegal pikes or rebellious carbines. In the *Canton de Vaud* I saw the Swiss farmers and mechanics practicing with their own sure rifles, not a soldier on guard to keep them from aiming at their rulers, and no holy water near to wet their republican primings.

CHAPTER XI.

PERSONS AND POLITICS IN DIVONNE.

Our society was composed for a time of simple citizens only, but a month or more after my arrival came some specimens of European nobility. They were the Countess of Manteuffel, with her son and daughter, Germans by descent, but Russians by nationality, belonging in one of those Sclavonic provinces on the Baltic which were anciently conquered and feudalized by adventurers of the Teutonic race. They bore no relationship to the famous Russian minister of the same name; their very armorial bearings were different. The elder countess was a lady of tall and stately form, with a mild dignity in her face and air, eyes of calm azure, and high, regular features, marking a beauty which must have been noticeable thirty years ago. She looked and stepped very nobly, yet very quietly and sweetly, although at the bottom of all there seemed to be a hidden spring of proud reserve.

The count, a man of twenty-five years, and his sister, two or three years younger, were very different from their mother. They showed ordinary round physiognomies, with blue, laughing eyes, curling hair, and brief noses. The brother was a quiet, plain-mannered man, a good fellow from the bottom of his heart, with no more air of pretension about him than if he had been born a shoeblack. His sister exactly resembled him in easy, kindly simplicity and unobtrusiveness.

One so little expects to see homely people do beautiful things, that I looked on with admiring wonder when an action of charming grace fell from this young countess.   In company with two or three other ladies, all busy over books or embroidery, she sat in the saloon one evening, unobservant that her mother had entered.   Mademoiselle Arnaud, a young Genevoise, rose, sprang to a chair, brought it to the table, and with a pretty gesture invited the elder countess to sit down by them.   The daughter rose also, but she had been anticipated.   Without a word, she went up to Mademoiselle Arnaud, bent down and kissed her cheek, then quietly resumed her place and her occupation. No hesitancy, no awkwardness, no ostentation appeared in this little tribute of thanks, which was as naturally given as it was conceived amiably.

These Manteuffels were fair specimens of the simpler and more unpretending class of European nobility.   I must do that style of humanity the justice to say that, as far as I had an opportunity of watching its manners, they were remarkable for nothing so much as naturalness and good taste.   I was surprised to find in them less haughtiness, less reserve, less affectation of superiority than in many of our own leading people, or even some few of the upper *bourgeoisie* of Europe. Pride incomparable there may be in the soul, but on the surface only a fascinating courtesy and unpretentiousness.   The Russian nobility have the reputation of being the haughtiest in manner, at the same time that they are the least ancient and most plebeian in origin.   A German noble is seldom troubled by fits of arrogance except when he thinks a commoner of his own nation is too presumptuous and persevering in his approaches. The English aristocracy, what very little I have seen of it, has a cold, quiet, passionless civility, which jars on no stranger's self-respect, and may conceal, Heaven knows what, of immeasurable haughtiness or sincere amiability. But of all nobilities that I have observed, the Italian seemed to me the most facile, sociable, unassuming. Wonderfully good-natured, good-for-nothing fellows are those bachelor counts and marquesses who haunt the cafés and drive on the promenades of Italian cities; talking about operas and ices, comedies and women; on bowing terms with every body, from the Grand-Duke to some insignificant clerk in the post-office; always idle and useless, always glad to be amused, always particularly civil to a foreigner. I remember one elderly Neapolitan duke, a man of real position and a respectable author, who was the most cozy, comfortable, chatty, inconsequential old gentleman that was ever perfectly at home in talk and sunshine. Such are my general impressions of the manners of European aristocracy, the best behaved class of humanity that I ever had the pleasure of observing.

Two families of the old country-nobility of France resided in our immediate neighborhood. About twenty rods from the Establishment, on a high, abrupt green knoll, which overlooked the village and the plain, stood the chateau of the Count of Divonne. It was a quadrangular modern building, like an ordinary country-house, with no pretensions to magnificence beyond its command over that majestic landscape; in short, a very unworthy successor to the knightly old castle

which it replaced, and of whose martial masonry a
fragment still peeped humbly from the garden wall.
The count himself was a kind of modern reconstruc-
tion, being, if I recollect right, only a cousin of the
direct line of the family.   I never heard him speak,
as he had few dealings with our Protestant doctor,
and none whatever with his Calvinistic invalids.   He
was a tall, dark man of about forty, of good appearance and grave manners.   He was anti-Republican, fervently Catholic, and his house was for some time the
home' of that famously troublesome Jesuit and exile,
the Bishop of Freiburg.   I inquired the income of this
French aristocrat, and was told that he might have
about four thousand dollars a year, which my inform-
ants seemed to consider a very pretty sum.

Our other feudal neighbor was a tall, stout, blond
man of about thirty, called Baron de Prés.   His chateau, a building as modern as the count's, and still
plainer in architecture, lay a mile and a half from the Establishment, just on the frontier of Switzerland.   The
baron had the healthy sunburn and large muscular
frame of the neighboring farmers of the Canton de Vaud.
He had been little in Paris, so that his manners and
talk had a provincial smack, reminding one much more
of a Swiss than a Frenchman; but his blood was really ancient, and his features had the true aristocratic
type, a Grecian inclining to aquiline.   His father distinguished himself on the insurgent side in the first
French Revolution, since which the family has always
been republican, or at least liberal, in politics.   Our
baron seemed to me one of the sensible men of France,
a moderate Democrat of the Cavaignac school, the only

set under whom the republic was possible. In manners he was rather shy of strangers, but a good fellow at heart, and a boisterous joker when cozily settled at the table of his crony the doctor.

Turning from an invalid aristocracy to our invalid plebeianism in the Establishment, I am arrested by a recollection of the Italian Caprini. A little slovenly fellow of twenty-four, with a venerable air, which appeared to consist in looking very snuffy and shuffy, he always seemed dirty in spite of his four washings a day, and was, on the whole, what might be called an ugly man, although his features were regular, his dark cheek flushed with color, and his eyes of a fine hazel. He spoke French pretty fluently, but with one of the strongest and most disagreeable accents in the world. On his alien lips the simplest sounds of the language withered into something outlandish and incomprehensible. *Chose* became *sose ;* and *argent, arzent.* Some of our Frenchmen, forbearing as that nation usually is to blunderers in its syntax, got out of all grammatical patience with Caprini, and used to badger him like schoolmasters about his heathenish dialogue. "My God !" said one of them, in a transport of impatience, "you are insupportable ; you have certain phrases that come from the other world."

Caprini, unlike the Piedmontese in general, was a supreme coward, and the mischievous set who haunted our billiard-room had several good jokes against him on the score of his sensitive nervous system. He sometimes visited Nyon, which was about six miles from Divonne, the road to it leading through a fine plain, well cultivated, and sprinkled with country-

seats.   A couple of our people were lounging along
this road about dusk, and had reached the shadow of
a small grove, through which shone the white walls
of a gentleman's country-residence, when from beyond
a turn in the route they heard footsteps approaching
in great haste.   In a moment more Caprini bolted
round the corner, holding a cocked pistol straight before him, and looking from right to left among the
trees with as much alarm as if, to his certain knowledge, the forty thieves had been hidden among the
peaceable and well-pruned foliage.   At sight of his
bath-fellows he gave a joyful shout, and ran forward
to meet them.   "What is the matter?" said they.
"What are you doing with that pistol?   Have you
seen any body?"

"Oh, nobody; but I thought it looked dangerous
in this forest; and then I was walking fast, and robbers always think you have money when you walk
fast; and so I took out my pistol to deter them from
an attack."

His hearers set up a shout of scornful laughter, and
told him that the country was as safe as a bath-tub.

A few days after this perilous adventure he had a
disagreement over a bet at billiards with a Frenchman
named Trocon, a pugnacious, powerful fellow, who
would have had no fear of settling the dispute corpo-
really, either with fists or pistols.   Frenchmen, however, seldom proceed to personal violence in their quar-
rels; usually, if the dispute can not be decided by
words, falling back quietly on the duel, so that the
Italian was quite safe from being cuffed by his Her-
culean opponent.   But as Trocon happened to be ab-

sent at Nyon the next day, our jokers got up a report that he had gone there to procure seconds and pistols, with the intention of washing out his affront in Caprini's blood. The most horrible accounts were circulated concerning his ferocity of temper, and his deadly feats of marksmanship in former grave affairs of the kind. The poor Italian fled from the now insufferable billiard-room, and sought consolation in pouring his tale of woe into my bosom. He had lost command over his French for the moment, and spoke in his native language. In an agony of stammering and trembling he pretended to take his fate coolly, and paraded a philosophical indifference to death. *"Cosa mi importa la vita?"* "What do I care for life?" said he, looking as if he would give his ears for an assurance that he should exist twenty-four hours longer. To my eternal honor, I was pitiful, and tried to convince him that our billiard-room jesters were only cracking a joke at his expense. At night Trocon came back from Nyon with no pistols, and laughed uproariously but pacifically when informed of the tales and terrors of the day.

Winter was now approaching, and my comrades began to take flight for their homes. The two brothers Monod left us, one after the other, each departure being a heavy drain on the interest and sprightliness of our society. I shall always remember, for another reason, when Frederick Monod went away, and that is, that I was then kissed for the first time by one of my own sex. *"À la Française,"* said this delightful pastor, and, before I recovered from my surprise, we had kissed each other on both cheeks. It was not so bad

E

as I had expected, but I can imagine that it would be much more agreeable to exchange the same salute with a woman.

Very strange it seems to Europeans of the Continent that, in England and America, men never bestow this token of affection on their male friends, and, above all, that it is never exchanged between male relations. "Queer people," said the doctor, talking of this subject. "An Englishman will not kiss his own brother."

"Yes," said Prince Georges L——, a Russian, "and, worse than that, a father in that chilly country will refuse to put his lips to the cheek of his son. The son has perhaps been in India twenty years; he comes home, and lands at London; they meet on the quay, and shake hands as if they had parted over night."

"Very unpleasant manners," rejoined the doctor. "And just notice how cold and discourteous they are to ladies. There is Mr. Reynolds, one of my patients, a man of learning, and, they say, a gentleman born; but see him meet our lady friends in the garden or by the fountains. He never says 'Good-morning;' he even passes them without raising his hat."

"But," interposed I, "Mr. Reynolds does not know all the ladies; he speaks to those he is acquainted with."

"But he ought to salute the others when he passes them; every body does it," insisted the doctor.

"No; there excuse me. Every body does it here, but not in England and America. More than that, you are not permitted there to salute a lady with whom you are not on speaking terms.   It would be considered an impertinence ; you would not be answered."

" What ! not when you were living under the same roof ?"

" Not even then."

" Well, there it is again," persisted the doctor. " The people are kind enough at heart, but iced all over in manners by their absurd reserve.   Give me something more civil in appearance, I say, even if there is not much soul in it."

During the autumn a great deal of rain fell, and December marked its passage by some light dashes of snow.   They were only temporary visitors from the top of the neighboring Jura, and usually degenerated into slush and mud within twenty-four hours ; but every week we could see the white drapery of the eastern peaks reaching farther down toward Leman, as if the prudent Alps were letting out the tucks in their winter garments.   As the frosts thickened around us, we garnished our feet with those huge wooden shoes, called *sabots,* so much worn by the French peasantry. I stared in amazement at my own pedals when I first saw them cased in those ponderous pieces of carpentry ; and I certainly never made such tracks before nor since as I then imprinted in the snowdrifts which thicker and thicker gathered over our deserted landscapes.   It costs time and pains (many pains) to get one's feet used to these whitewood slippers, even with the protection of an interior sock of woven list ; but they are necessities, for, except in large cities, India-rubbers are unknown on the Continent, and ordinary shoeing was no match for the wear and wet of hydrop-

athy in a Juratic winter; for into the winter I was
steadily going, under a full sail of moist sheets and
towels, as heroic in pursuit of health as a Nantucket
whaler in chase of polaric blubber.   I was still gaining on my malady, but not so rapidly as at Graefenberg, perhaps because I was now very near the far-
thest limits of recovery, and it was therefore harder to
improve.

In one object of my residence in a French Water-
cure—that is, in acquiring the language—I had been
even more successful than I anticipated.   Without
numerous and excellent letters of introduction, I could
not possibly have obtained otherwheres and otherwise
so much good society as I found at Divonne.   It is
vexatious to an American to discover how long he may
live in a city of the Continent, and yet have occasion
to address none of its inhabitants except coachmen,
waiters, and other persons whose grammar and conversation are equally unedifying.   Boarding-houses at
Paris, for instance, are almost unknown; and those
two or three which exist are filled with Anglo-Saxons,
who come there in the hope of talking French, but
talk only English.   At the hotels you meet travelers
and transient natives, who stay but a night or so, and
with whom you form no intimacy.   But at Divonne,
in a week's time, I found myself on sociable terms with
fifty people, nearly all well educated, and some of them
belonging to the best classes of European society.   Reserve would have been difficult in our circumstances,
and no one had the bad taste to attempt it.   Thus I
heard at Divonne not only better French than would
have been vouchsafed to me at Paris, but more in a

week than I should have heard there in a month.
During about four months, indeed, I spoke no other
language, not meeting in that period a solitary Englishman or American. The consequence of all this
was a facile acquisition of words and accent which
surprised me, and won numberless eulogiums from my
native acquaintance. My object in noting these circumstances is to show Americans abroad where to
learn a foreign tongue, and how. Not in the unsocial
populousness of great cities; not by taking bachelor
lodgings and dining at the restaurants; but at some
table d'hôte, where you meet from day to day the same
faces, and, best of all, when such a table can be found
in the freedom of a country resort.

To get along faster on my grammatical stilts (for
thus awkward are the first steps in a foreign tongue),
I took a teacher, a young man, the clerk of the village lawyer. He was not of the best quality, for he
had something of the accent of the district; and, in addition, he was entirely unaccustomed to the style of foreigners in French, so that my idioms often puzzled
him to that degree that he could hardly tell whether
they were right or wrong. But he was useful in making me write regularly, as also in giving me conversational practice, after my fellow-patients had mostly departed. He used to come every afternoon, in his suit
of plain gray, and sit for an hour or two over my comfortable stove, discussing the composition of the morning, and closing with a miscellaneous talk on all things
and some others. One day our tongues rambled on
to the state of the commonwealths of South America.
"I suppose," said he, " that you will seize upon those

countries some day.   They are devilishly behindhand
(*diablement en arrière*), and want somebody to start
them on."   The expression amused me.

Politics was our favorite subject, especially French
politics, and its different phases in struggling toward
a true and steady Republicanism.   He believed in the
Republic; at all events, passionately hoped in it; and
he looked forward to another outburst in the spring—
a new strife for a complete liberty, which should altogether triumph.   "Do not resume your travels for
some months," said he; "our elections come on soon,
and then there will be a rising.   When France rises,
Europe rises; and you will not then find a country
near us in which you can travel safely.   Here you
are not in danger, but it would be different in Paris or
in the cities of Italy.   When the people strikes again
it will punish the traitors, and by mistake you might
fall in some dark night for another."

Whether he said this from a knowledge of the plots
which were then weaving to entangle the Prince-President, or whether he was simply a looker-on in Venice,
and but talked on guess-work, I never asked him and
never knew.   An answer was preparing to his oracle
such as he little expected.

On the fourth of December, 1852, as the half a doz-
en patients who still remained were sitting down to
dinner, the Swiss pastor Berteau walked into the
room, holding out a *Journal des Débats* just from
Paris.   His fine lips curled contemptuously under his
jetty beard, and his black eyes flashed with a strange
mixture of scorn and anger.   Swiss and Republican to
the bottom of his soul; proud of his national liberty

as Lucifer of his morning supremacy, he grasped in his hand the condemnation of a people which had tried in vain to be free. " Hurrah for the Republic !" he said, in a fierce, contemptuous tone, and flung the journal on the table before the doctor.

" What do you mean ?" asked the other, with a stare of vague inquietude.

" Hurrah for the Republic ! Read there," repeated Berteau, placing his finger on a passage of two or three lines at the bottom of a column. The doctor raised the paper and read aloud this announcement: " Paris is in a state of siege. The National Assembly is dissolved. The streets are occupied by troops."

A veil of sudden, hopeless dismay fell on every countenance. There was an expectation, a silence, a turning of the head to see if any one were near. A few words, very few, expressed the astonishment, and fewer still the wrath of the auditors. Even in that distant republican corner of France the *coup d'état* was received unresisted, undenounced, in stupor, and in terror. Directly opposite me sat a man who for weeks past had been openly swearing vengeance against the enemies of French liberty, and prophesying an imminent hour when they should be swept into sudden nothingness. Not a word now passed his lips at this condemnation of his hopes ; and after the first stare of amazement, he never lifted his eyes from his food. It seemed as if every hand were paralyzed by unseen manacles, and every head bent toward the glitter of the guillotine by an irresistible fascination, as flowers are drawn toward the brightness of the sun. This man—this Red Republican, who sat

before me, rose from the table speechless, and lived for
weeks thereafter in a silent terror greater than his
noisy confidence of before.

The day following we heard that our Republican
friend, Baron de Prés, had fled across the frontier to
the Swiss village of Crassy. Trocon, my teacher, and
I made him a visit, and found him in a hired room,
with a good look-out toward France, and three or four
rifles and fowling-pieces standing loaded in one corner.
" Here I am," said he, " running away from the *coup
d'état.* I was in no particular danger, that I know
of ; but my opinions are understood, and I thought it
best to be on the safe side of the frontier. There is
no telling what fancies a prefect of police might take
to one in a time like this. But I tell you one thing,
Trocon ; we must all turn Protestants. France will
never be free as long as these cursed priests rule the
souls of our population. Hereafter I mean to go pretty often to the Protestant church, if it is only to spite
the shaved devils. Sacred name of names ! it is the
sole revenge they have left us. And to think of being
fooled in this way by an idiot—a dull, slow ass—an
accident. This Louis Napoleon is not a man ; he is
only an event. Well, events succeed each other ; I
am waiting for ours."

Good reader, Catholic reader, reactionist reader, suffer the baron to rail, or even swear, in the bitterness
of his disappointment and the foam of his impotent
wrath. He has been cheated of his republic, and
rendered for years to come a suspected man, whose
rise is impossible except on the smoky wings of hy-
pocrisy. He sits in a hired apartment on foreign soil,

looking at his lands and chateau, without daring to pluck the fruit of the one or darken the threshold of the other.   He knows that thousands who believe as he does are thus situated, and even as much worse off as prison and death can make them, solely that Louis Napoleon may reign unmolested.   Let him rave.

News soon came of fighting in Paris, barricades hastily thrown up, desperate struggles on the *Boulevards*, alternations of victory and defeat.   The hopes of our village Republicans were raised only to be dashed harder to earth.   We learned that the troops remained faithful to the usurper, and the usurper faithful in audacity and energy to himself.   A letter came to a young villager from his brother, a soldier in the garrison of Lyons.   "We are drunk all the while," he wrote; "the men get double pay; the officers have received large presents according to their grades."

Reports followed that a rising, sullied by deep atrocities, had taken place along the frontier districts bordering on western Switzerland and Savoy; that one department was entirely in the hands of the insurrectionists, and that the fire was creeping from valley to valley of that wooded and broken country.   Then came news of marchings of troops, provincial prisons full of Republicans, and a corpse-like quiet in the population.

Over the ruinous track of the *coup d'état* came the lying elections, like a mirage succeeding to a simoom. Fountains, rivers, oceans of liberty were advertised, and the people of France was driven up to satisfy its thirst for liberty at a ballot-box as densely surrounded by bayonets as a spring by bulrushes.   Eighty soldiers

E 2

of the line watched the freemen of our village as they
tremblingly exercised the glorious right of suffrage.
Billets marked *Oui* were printed for those who were
in favor of making Louis Napoleon President for ten
years, billets marked *Non* for those who did not think
him worthy of that considerable proof of confidence.
I observed that the latter were so distinguished by a
black line around the edge that they could not possibly
be folded in a manner to have them mistaken for the
others.   The Count of Divonne sat by the ballot-box,
sternly noting every man who deposited a lined billet;
and it was thought an act of immense hardihood when
Trocon, my Republican friend, laid down a broad, undisguised *Non*.   Our village, well known as violently
Liberal, if not Red, gave a large majority of *votes* for
the Prince-President.   How many of these patriotic
Ouis were the suffrages of the Count of Divonne, and
how many were deposited by men who neither dared
vote otherwise nor stay away, would be a curious
problem, difficult of solution.

One of the leading lawyers of Gex, a small city
about eight miles from Divonne, undertook to distribute billets of *Non* to his fellow-citizens.   The Prefect
of Police sent for him, and received him with an air of
grim confidence.   "I understand, Monsieur Leroux,"
said he, "that you are distributing billets of *Non*."

"It is true, Monsieur the Prefect.   I believe that
I have a constitutional right to do so."

"Oh, certainly, Monsieur ; no one disputes your
right.   But allow me to observe that, if you distribute
any more of them, the consequences may be very unpleasant to yourself, Monsieur Leroux — extremely

unpleasant. Observe, Monsieur," continued the prefect, taking a pinch of snuff, and looking the lawyer steadily in the eyes, "I do not wish to interfere with your liberty; I only forewarn you of a very probable and very disagreeable result to the continuance of your present conduct. Good-day, Monsieur Leroux. I have the honor to salute you."

Leroux himself told me this story, and frankly acknowledged that, from fear of those evil consequences so plainly hinted at by the friendly official, he took care to be seen with no more bundles of negative billets in his Republican fingers.

I asked my teacher if the immense mass of peasantry had not Democratic principle enough to rise against such contemptuous menaces and cajoleries. "But," said he, "they know nothing about it. How should they? They have had no political education. They say, 'Oh, we must have some one there at Paris.' They would vote for a king under a republic, and not know that they had committed a contradiction. For the rest, they will obey the priests."

Such were the elections with which Louis Napoleon attempted to drape his usurpation. France may have fallen lower at other times, but she never fell more ridiculously. It was bad enough to be beaten thus like a hound; but to be forced to gambol and wag her tail under the rod was ludicrously contemptible.

CHAPTER XII.

WINTER IN DIVONNE.

SUBSEQUENT to the bustle of those farcical elections came several months remarkable for little to me besides winter and loneliness.   The patients of Divonne were not hardened to cold by the enthusiasm of the Graefenbergers, so that only two braves, Trocon and I, remained to encounter the inclemency of January packings and douches.   The climate of the Valley of Geneva is not at any season of the year a very perfect one, except in two or three sheltered nooks like Montreuil; while in winter it is boisterous and glacial enough to make a white bear curse the north pole, and wish himself at the equator.   No great quantity of snow fell—not more, perhaps, at any one time than five or six inches; but from the Jura and the opposite Alps descended a frozen breath which neutralized our warmest noontide.   Sometimes for a week together the air was gray with a chilly fog, rendering the immense surrounding peaks as invisible as if they had no existence, sheeting the whole lower landscape like a spectral shroud, freezing with a slow persistency, and gradually covering every branch, and twig, and frostbitten herb with an icy filigree, until, when the sun came out, the valley seemed like a fairy land, opulent with forests of feathery silver fruiting into diamonds.   Then the *bise*, or north wind, rushed furiously down from the upper end of the lake, replacing the still, dull frigidity of the mist by an equal monotony of whistling blasts, chill, strong, and unwearying.

This *bise* is about the same thing as the *mistral* of Marseilles, which is said to blow something like fourteen days out of every week. Its favorite place of bustle around Lake Leman is the city of Geneva, which, being situated at the bottom of the valley, where it narrows very nearly to the breadth of the Rhone, is about as much exposed to gusts as if it were in the nozzle of a bellows. A torrent of dust often crowds its narrow streets, scouring in at the northern side of the city and out at the southern, like a current of mad emigration, tending toward some humid bourne in Mediterranean billows. I never in my life wore my hat tighter on my head, nor got more gravel and dust in my eyes, than during my visits to Geneva.

Notwithstanding atmospheric observations and linguistic studies, I sometimes felt dreadfully lonely and unemployed in my hydropathic seclusion. Even Trocon was at one time absent for more than a week. The reader can imagine how hard pushed I was for amusement when I tell him that I once passed five minutes very agreeably in making faces at a strange cat, who had perched himself on the outer window-sill to observe the solitude of the saloon. The animal stared in undisguised amazement until the spectacle apparently became too harrowing for endurance, when he disappeared with a scared jump, like a rustic frightened by a ghost.

Another means of diversion was Trompette, a good-natured, good-for-nothing, loafing specimen of a bushy-tailed small dog. As white as a dirty dog could be, shaggy and uncombed, with short legs, a tongue that was too long for him, a very neatly turned peroration, and lively red eyes, he looked like a quadruped of character. A sharp dog he was for cutting summersets; skillful at playing toss up and catch with lumps of sugar; remarkable also for whining lamentably in tune to the church bells. It was his misfortune to have fleas, but not his fault, I am sure, for he took the most vigorous measures to get rid of them. He would bite madly at his populous back, then roll himself desperately in the gravel, then take to his heels with such swiftness as to leave his tail behind him (an inch or so), then halt to nibble again as if he meant to eat himself up entirely. On account of this misfortune, Trompette was not a welcome guest in the house, and seldom dared enliven it with his flea-bitten presence, so that whenever he was admitted he took it as a rare favor, turning summersets of gratitude, and wagging his tail as indefatigably as a pendulum. If allowed to remain to dinner, he took post by the chair of the most charitable person in the company, but held himself prepared to follow up any other chance prospect of an immediate morsel. His head awry, and one eye cocked at you like a chicken, he watched every bit in its transit from the plate to your mouth with an anxiety which he made no attempt to conceal; and when it finally disappeared in that orifice where bits (whether horses' or other bits) usually go, he licked his chops involuntarily, as if from instinctive sympathy (somewhat envious) with your happiness. He evidently had not strength of mind to tear himself from this unprofitable spectacle, the most aggravating species of misery, perhaps, of which a doggish nature is capable.

During the month of warm weather which I saw at Divonne, Trompette enjoyed himself beyond description in the sunshine. Couching in the sultriest noontide, he sunk into a luxurious dream-life, sometimes waking up with a start at the sensation of a fly on his nose or a flea in his ear, exerting his lazy faculties for a moment to bite or shake off the enemy of his peace, then spreading himself again to the sun, so sweltering, so toasted that he was all but ready to pop, like a chestnut in the ashes. And all this while there was a remarkably shrewd, self-satisfied air about him, as though he would have said, " If I ain't a watch-dog, I know the time of day ; if I ain't a pointer, I am a keen dog at all points ; my nose is rather to the point, I fancy, and so are my ears ; there is health in my bark, and waggishness in my tail."

Our establishment also boasted a pet lamb, who vanished mysteriously about the beginning of winter, and whom I supposed to have been killed and eaten, as usually happens at last to the respectable part of the woolly population. But on one of the early warm days of spring he reappeared, now grown up to sheephood ; and, emerging from the stable, where he had passed the cold weather among the cows and horses, proceeded to divert himself by stepping on the flower-beds, munching the oleanders and rose-bushes, butting at Trompette and the hens, until, having done mischief enough in an hour to satisfy a reasonable sheep for a week, he was finally chased back to his stall by the outraged gardener. Two or three repetitions of this foray generally exhausted the patience of the doctor, who would then cause Bunty to be tied up again in the stable, and thus force him to let the hens and oleanders alone for a season.

I must bequeath a page or so to the memory of my particular friend and boon companion in the revels of hydropathy, Monsieur Trocon. He was a middle-sized Frenchman of thirty-three or thereabouts, with heavy shoulders, a broad chest, and immense muscles; in short, a perfect model of those fine fellows whom one sees about France in the red trowsers of the Zouaves or the blue tunics of the Chasseurs ; just the kind of man to leap up the fire-swept precipices of the Alma, or to struggle with a heroic vitality through the fatigues and privations of a Crimean winter. He had served a while in the artillery, where his reckless temper and wild love of pleasure had several times brought him into difficulties, and at last forced him to buy himself out in order to escape the severity of his officers. He considered it curious, and, in fact, rather humorous, that the man who replaced him was finished, a short time after, by the well-aimed bullet of an Arab in Algeria.

Having rid himself of cannon and sabre exercise, he turned his attention to getting a living, and when I knew him was a very respectable and well-to-do carriage-maker. It was actually a disappointment in love which shook his colossal constitution, and sent him for health to the restorative humidities of Divonne. Once there, he became fascinated by the cure, and precipitated himself into a dissipation of packings and sitz-baths. At one time the doctor sent him away, telling him that he was well; but in a week he was back again, declaring that his life hung by a thread. The thread in question would probably have served a Brobdignag tailor, for at this very time he was a kind of enormity of muscular force. In fact, he had got hypped, and imagined himself sick, in consequence of having been too well all the early part of his life. Many a man who has lived thirty years in perfect health believes himself going into a decline on the first attack of stomach-ache.

Whether a Frenchman has more vanity than an American or an Englishman, I do not know; but, at all events, he takes the liberty to show more of it in his conversation. He is apt to talk copiously about himself, analyze at large his own peculiarities of character, and conclude himself, on the whole, to be a good fellow. I have heard French-women describe most minutely, particularize even to hair-splitting, their sentiments toward men whom they had loved, or supposed they had loved. On the other hand, I may notice that the French are very charitable to this sociable egotism in other people, and listen to a fellow-mortal's expatiations on himself without impatience, without reproaching him, even behind his back, for self-conceit. What seems to us vanity may be in part only a greater degree of frankness and communicativeness.

Trocon had this characteristic of discussing himself as minutely as if he was a delicate *plat*, or a question before the Assemblée Nationale. If any one remonstrated with him on some unreasonable habit or prejudice, he would give, as an all-sufficient explanation, "That's my way" (*Je suis comme ça*). This robust and self-reliant reason was good for every thing, from his peculiarity of hating priests and aristocrats worse than he hated the devil, down to his other peculiarity of eating boiled eggs for breakfast in contradiction of all rules of hydropathic diet. In exact truth, his was an instinctive nature, abominating things because they were uncongenial, and loving them because they were sympathetic. A downright French character it was—very much resembling the Irish; more moved by emotion than by reason; vigorous rather than persevering. In politics and religion his sentiments were on the right side; Nature had made him a hater of despotism, whether monarchic or priestly. But, with this passionate energy as a motor of action, he would, I think, have been a reckless man in success, a famous fellow for heads and confiscations. If not an absolute "Red," he was something more than light pink or rose color. I have seen him shake his iron fist and howl like a wild beast as the flushed, haughty face, and tranquil, assured step of the Bishop of Freiburg passed our door. The *coup d'état* fell upon him like a personal misfortune; it broke his sleep, made him melancholy and almost sick.

His revolutionary tastes showed themselves early, or rather, perhaps, were formed by an incident which occurred in his boyhood. At fourteen he was an apprentice in a workshop at Paris, when, some umbrage having been excited by the new government of Louis Philippe, the blouses resorted to their favorite political measure of barricades and arms. Little Trocon picked up a musket and cartridge-box in the street, and, concluding that it was a free fight, counted himself in without ceremony. " I found myself with some other workmen from the shop," said he, " and we fired upon all the soldiers we could see. Sometimes we ran away from the dragoons, and sometimes I thought I had lived my last day. Then we would take a new post around some corner, and shoot at them down the street. I can not say if I hit any body or not, for there was such a dust and hurry that I hardly saw any thing. And during all that time there I never knew what I was fighting for. If any one had said to me, Trocon, what wantest thou? I would not have known what to reply. But how we fought those beggars of soldiers! My God! I laugh when I think of it."

That scene occurred over twenty years ago, but the outlines and coloring for such another exist to-day. If a revolution should happen to-morrow in Paris, hundreds of little Trocons, just as indifferent to motives, just as heedless of results, would man the barricades, and fight like heroes and ignoramuses. The plebeians of Rome, the blouses of Paris, the b'hoys of New York, the filibusters of New Orleans, are the same race, and, morally speaking, live in the same country, the same epoch.

Trocon had fought a duel, too, which he described somewhat in the following style: " I was living in Paris then; I was a man grown, and knew life a little. There arrived there a young fellow from my place, who looked me up. As he was the son of an old friend of our family, I made him see the city, and did my best to divert him. One evening we took chairs outside of the Café Tortoni, and demanded something—I have forgotten what now—but coffee and brandy perhaps. Close by us were a couple of officers — lieutenants — fellows just risen from the ranks, I suppose—real bears.   One of them wanted a light for his cigar, and, instead of asking it of the waiter, he turned upon my friend and lighted from him—without asking permission, mark you, or even touching his hat.   My young fellow got all red; but, being no more than a boy, and not knowing life, he said nothing.   I took the matter up there.   ' Monsieur,' said I, ' that is not the manner of a gentleman who lights his cigar.'   He regarded me very impertinently, and said, ' It seems to me that that concerns your comrade, and not you.'   I replied, ' Monsieur, I make it concern me; my friend, being a stranger here, is under my protection, and I demand that you make your apology to him.'   Eh! well; one word led to another, and, in fine, it was decided that we should finish it with the pistol. The morning after, we encountered each other early in the Wood of Boulogne.   It fell to him by lot to fire the first.   He raised his pistol, pulled, and never hit me. Then I pulled, and, my God! I never hit him neither. Eh! well; that ended the affair, and I have never seen the beggar since."

At Divonne, Trocon came very near being involved in a duel with one of the officers of the little garrison. After the *coup d'état* he cut the acquaintance of the priest of the village, that being the only sacrifice of revenge which he could accord to his outraged country. Happening to meet the reverend gentleman promenading with a lieutenant who was a mutual friend, he passed them both without a recognition, unwilling to let the priest suppose that even half of a bow was meant for him.   The lieutenant was incensed, demanded explanations, received the above reason, declared it unsatisfactory, insisted upon apologies to himself and his reverend friend. His brother officers, including the captain, were called in, and, rather curiously, decided against him. He ungraciously accepted the assertions of Trocon that no personal offense was intended, and lived on very ceremoniously bearish terms with him thereafter.

Another acquaintance, of the same political creed as Trocon, but very different from him in character, was a Frenchman whom I shall call Jolivet, a tall, slender man, American rather than French in his build, and somewhat American, too, in his slow tones and lounging manner. In opinions he was a radical progressive, doubting the old creeds of religion, doubting the existing forms of society, looking confidently to something new, something better—in short, to the onward march and ultimate perfection of humanity. As I was orthodox in religion, and believed society in the present shape of the family to be the only society possible, we never talked on these subjects without disputing. Like infidels in general, he kept his temper admirably, made his assertions cautiously, and had rather the air of an inquirer after truth than a preacher of any particular dogma. I, on the contrary, after the fashion of most people who imagine that they have Heaven on their side, was apt to be positive in my assertions and very crushing in my denunciations. I was startled and shocked at his quiet denials of what I had been educated to consider sacred truths, and I had not always the self-possession to remember that I must prove that these truths were sacred before I could demand his respect for them. He, on the other hand, free from any educational belief (often more obstinate and violent than a reasoned one), and resting in that tranquil nonentity of faith which Rousseau calls a state of respectful doubt, had no prejudices to wound, no fixed positions to defend, and so kept his temper unmoved in the controversy. As he never at first stated his opinions broadly, but allowed me gradually to draw them out of him, I was some time in discovering his exact credence. "Why, then," I said to him at last, "you are no more nor less than an atheist."

"Excuse me : not at all. I believe in God."

"But you are, at least, infidel to the Christian religion."

"Let me explain. I believe somewhat in the divine nature of Jesus, as I believe that all noble and superior souls partake largely of the divine intellect and goodness. If you speak of the Christian religion as it is commonly stated, I acknowledge that I am incredulous of that. The fall and the redemption—I deny them, I admit it."

It was the second time in my life that I had heard so frank a declaration of infidelity, and I stared in some naïve astonishment at its hardihood. As the discussion went on, I fell back upon that proof of Christianity which exists in the interior spiritual life of the devout. And here I showed my ignorance of human nature and of the intimate history of religions in general by asserting that this inward piety, these seemingly supernatural emotions, are confined entirely to Christians, and almost altogether to Protestants.

"Allow me to doubt that," said he, with his usual

cold tone and courteous manner. "I am inclined to think that the Moslems and Brahmins experience those phenomena, and I know that they exist abundantly among Catholics. Only our revelations take a character from our education just as yours from your education; and as you have sublime emotions concerning Christ and the fathers, so do ours seem to descend from the Virgin and the saints. I can tell you something of that from my own experience. I was educated for a priest. A mere boy of sixteen, I was surrounded by holy fathers, and believed fervently all that they taught me. I used to pray constantly, and fast often, to gain these spiritual enlightenments; and I fancied that I received them. I sometimes had raptures—ecstasies of devotional feeling; and once or twice came visions of the Virgin, urging me to struggle toward heaven. But all this passed away as circumstances changed and the priestly influences around me declined. I am convinced that these spiritual impressions are nothing but the effects of education acting on a fervent and impressible imagination. You see that I have had this interior life that you adduce as a proof of Christianity, and without result on my belief. Your appeal fails, therefore; we must return to our reasoning."

Such was a specimen of Jolivet's conversation on points of religious credence. With regard to theories on society, he had reached exactly the same limit—a negation of the justice of what existed, but no positive idea of what will be or should be. He often read socialistic books, but I could not find that he put faith in any one of them. He attached little importance

to Fourier's system of phalansteries, and had no similar plan of his own to propose.   But he had a firm
assurance that something would yet be found gentler
than the family, stronger than the police, broader than
Republicanism, which would give quiet to humanity,
and well-being to every one of its members.   I maintained that, as far as possible, the individual should
be left free, unassisted by law, as well as untrammeled
by it.   I adduced America as the country where this
idea was carried fullest into action, and challenged
him to produce a land in which society is more stable
or prosperity more equally divided.

"I have no immense admiration for your state of
things in America," he replied.   "It is superficial and
temporary.   It derives from this, that you have ten
times more land than you want, and therefore easily
raise food enough for every one.   You would be im-
beciles, and less than men, if you failed to do so.   But
build cities of a million inhabitants, crowd your country with four hundred souls to the square mile, and
you will have as much wretchedness as England or
France.   We want something better than this—something more humane than mere individualism—something more powerful than mere democracy.   I consider America behind France in a true view of the social
question.   You are satisfied with your present system, although it simply works well from temporary
circumstances which are fast passing away.   You will
not reach our discoveries until your masses are as pov-
erty-stricken as ours.   We have long ago lived clear
through your social existence, and are commencing, I
hope, a new era.   We have finished with your brute

well-being, your happiness of bread and meat, and
have begun to think out a reform which shall suit humanity in all its stages of progress and perfection. A
hundred years hence America will be forced to tread
in our footsteps. By then we may have placed things
on some true basis. God knows. It is a hard thing
to overturn prejudices of six thousand years' standing."

France is full of men wandering blindly and anxiously up and down the steps of socialistic platforms.
Even the brother of our doctor, although in general
nothing worse than a good Republican, threw out at
least one idea tinged with Fourierism. "Property,"
says Proudhon, "is robbery." My friend only went
so far as to say, "Retail is robbery." The merchant,
he averred, buys at one rate, and sells to the consumer
at an advanced rate; therefore he picks the consumer's pocket of all the difference between the two rates,
which is clearly robbery; and as the mass of consum-
ers are poor men, this robbery is doubly unprincipled,
because cruel. It was of no use to reply that, if it
were not for the merchant, the poor man would have
to go to China for his tea and to Cuba for his sugar,
which in the end would be more expensive than even
a large commission to the retailer. "The government," he said, "might see to that. There ought to
be vast magazines where merchandise should be re-
tailed at wholesale prices."

Strange to say, Trocon took my view of the subject; and, stranger still, a French Legitimist noble
sided with my antagonist. We had a long dispute,
in which we talked vociferously, and, after the man-

F

ner of Frenchmen, all together, nobody taking the
trouble to listen to the opposite party.   As usual in
discussions, not a soul was convinced; and we ended,
like dancers in a quadrille, with each one occupying
his first position.

CHAPTER XIII.

SPRING IN DIVONNE.

As spring returned, the giant landscape around us freshened into verdure, while the atrocious *bise* diminished its chilliness and frequency, until Divonne became a pleasanter place than I had yet imagined it. New company also began to arrive, cheering me even more than the young flowers, the gushings of bird-music, and the lengthened days of summer. sky.

The harbinger of this featherless flock of spring water-fowl was the Count de G——, a Frenchman of about twenty-eight, whom I soon discovered to be one of the most fanatical hydropaths that ever performed the douche-dance. It was perfectly in the character of the man, an enthusiast in every thing, a zealous Papist, a passionate anti-Republican, a loyal subject of Henri Cinq, a scorner of every political thing in France which was not old regime Legitimist. Yet, aristocrat in feeling and in blood as he was, he fell readily into our burgess society, not even holding himself aloof from radical, coach-building Monsieur Trocon. He was too sociable to be distant, too well-bred to assume superiority ; and then there was a bond between us which in his eyes was almost equal to nobility : that bond was the brotherhood of hydropathy, for which his respect was indescribable. He had been at Graefenberg, and, when he mentioned the circumstance, I remembered having seen him figure in the balls there, although I then supposed, from his fair complexion and tall form, that he was an Englishman or an American.

In his company I enjoyed the excitement of being arrested three times by the patrolling gendarmes who protected our frontier of France from the machinations of Republicans and sinners. It is my belief that these inquests were chiefly provoked by the uncivilized costume in which the count chose to pursue his watery labors. Without hat, without cravat, tramping through the mud and rain of early spring in a suit of brown linen, he certainly looked like a " vagrom man fit to be comprehended." In consequence of his promptings, as well as of my own Graefenberg education, I also fell into the scarecrow mode of dressing, and so shared his annoyances. Walking one day bareheaded through a drizzling rain, we were met about half a mile from the Swiss frontier by a tall, powerful trooper, a splendid specimen of the French *sabreur*, wearing the uniform of the mounted *gendarmerie*. He fixed the broad glare of his full hazel eye upon us, turning his head after us as we passed, and finally, checking his horse, called out, "Gentlemen, wait one instant."

We stopped and faced him. " Where are you going?" he continued.

" We are taking a walk," replied the count, rather contemptuously, as he resumed his march toward the land of freedom.

" Stop where you are!" shouted the trooper, spurring his horse past us, and placing himself across our route. " Now tell me where you are going and whence you come."

" We come from the village back here, and we are walking for exercise."

" You have not the air of belonging in such a village as this, and you are not dressed like people who are simply taking a walk. Gentlemen, you will please follow me before the mayor of Divonne. I wish to hear what he says of you."

" This is nonsense and insolence," said the count, getting angry; "I do not choose to be interrupted in my amusements in this style, and you have no right to do it, no authority to make an arrest."

" Monsieur, this department is under martial law. I am a sergeant of the military police, and my orders are to arrest every person who has the air of a suspicious character. You will have the goodness to walk before me to the village."

" I shall do nothing of the sort," said the count, making a resolute push to get by our officious friend. The sergeant gave his bridle a dexterous turn, and, hitting my comrade with the horse's flank, nearly flung him into a ditch which bordered the road. Obstinacy was clearly useless; the trooper was determined to know us better, and two old umbrellas were no match for pistols and a long sabre; besides which, it was supper-time, or very nearly. Wheeling about, we meekly retraced our steps toward Divonne, keeping pace with the fast-walking, powerful steed of our guardian. The count was overboiling with scornful rage, which he expressed in a series of bantering remarks, addressed to me, but meant to excoriate the sensibilities of the trooper. Johnny Darme got mad at the sarcasms, and was puzzled by the indifference we exhibited to

our fate; he tried to respond cuttingly, but by the
time we had reached the outskirts of the village he
was anxious to get rid of us. Meeting a squad of
youngsters who were chasing each other in their
clumsy *sabots* through the outskirting puddles of Divonne, he pulled up and inquired, with a despairing
effort at dignity, "My children, do you know these
gentlemen?"

"Oh yes, we see them every day," responded the
little fellows, with a stare of unlimited astonishment.

"It is well," declared the trooper; "that suffices
me.   Gentlemen, I bid you good-day."

"Good-day," said the count, with a smile of indignation; "Good-day," said I, with the sarcastic civility
of a man who wishes somebody better luck another
time; and the mortified sergeant, driving spurs into
his beast, plunged forward through the sloughy streets
to a station of *gendarmerie* in the centre of the village.
As it was now too late to continue our walk, we marched
straight to the Establishment, where the history of our
adventure was received with roars of laughter.

"I must have a reform in the costume of my patients," said the doctor.   "Why, the devil! it is
scandalous to have them trooping about in such style
as to be taken up for Socialists and vagrant Republicans."

"Excellent!" said his father-in-law, a jolly, red-
faced Genevese.   "I can not, for my part, imagine
why he let you go at all.   The trooper found that you
were not running away.   Well, what of that?   It
was clearly his duty to take you to some Bedlam or

other, and have you put out of the way of doing harm to sane people."

A few days after this, as we were wandering near the chateau of Baron de Prés, we were arrested by a gendarme on foot. He, too, wanted to know our names and conditions, where we were going, and what was our business in the country ; and he was particularly incredulous of our being in a hydropathic establishment at that ungenial season of the year. The count's genteel address and elegant accent bore passable witness to his respectability. The gendarme turned to me. "You are an Italian," he said, in a positive way.

"No ; excuse me, I am not in the least Italian."

"But you have a certain Italian accent, I am pretty sure."

"Very possibly. I learned Italian before French, and my first lessons in French were from an Italian master."

"Of what nation are you, then ?"

"An American, at your service."

"What is an American doing here ? Taking the cure also ? Do you come all the way from America to practice hydropathy in Divonne ?"

"Not precisely ; but, being here, I seized the opportunity."

"I know something of Doctor Vidart. Tell me a little about his house and family. I shall know whether you are describing with exactness."

I accordingly portrayed our doctor's respectable physique, followed up with an account of his wife and brother, and closed with a particular narration of the names, ages, and appearance of his children. "Very well," said the gendarme, with a grin; and, dropping his steady eye, which he had fixed hitherto on mine, he left us with a salute.

A week or two later, the count, Trocon, and I borrowed the doctor's carriage, and drove over to the little city of Gex. Lounging about its irregular streets, we came upon a station of *gendarmerie*, and were immediately arrested in a body by those entertaining people. They were uncommonly polite this time, and only insisted on having our names and conditions, by way of souvenir, in their little album. The count and Trocon were easily written down, but my position was rather more difficult to define. The stumpy, red-faced old sergeant had no suspicion that I was a foreigner, and my French name was not calculated to undeceive him. "Your place of residence?" said he.

"Connecticut."

"What?" he asked, bringing his chirography to a full stop, and looking me full in the face.

"Con-nect-i-cut."

"In what department?" said he, with an air of suspicion.

"The gentleman is an American," observed the count, "and Connecticut is a province of the United States."

"Ah! really!" said the old fellow, and asked for my passport immediately. Then, after two or three ineffectual attempts to repeat the name of my native state, he wrote it out, I have no idea with what orthographical success, and told us that we might go.

Among the earliest arrivals of spring were two Rus-

sian princes, brothers, Eugene and Georges L——, not
Germans by race, like the Manteuffels, but unmixed
and indigenous Muscovites. Eugene, the eldest, was
a man of about thirty-seven, small and dark, with gentle manners and a thoughtful expression, which changed
when he spoke into a lively good-humor. Georges,
seven or eight years younger, was very different : fair
complexioned, with stern blue eyes, irregular Northern
features, lofty stature, and a military air verging on
haughtiness. His wife, a tall and proud blonde, was
excessively vain of him, and assured me that I might
consider him the model of a handsome Russian. The
wife of the elder brother, also fair and blue-eyed, but
small, resembled her husband in the quiet amiability
of her expression and manners.

These people entered easily into our little circle, and
soon presented, at least to me, one of the most interesting features in its cosmopolitan variety. Even
Eugene's little boy, a child of three years old or thereabouts, was a character worth observing, inasmuch as
he understood three languages—English, French, and
Russian—but obstinately refused to utter a word of
any one of them. I suspect that he was dumbfounded by the large choice of expressions offered him, and
preferred waiting till he had discovered which lingo
best suited his infantile necessities. The parents were
naturally afraid that he might be dumb, and consulted
the doctor anxiously concerning the little fellow's taci-
turnity. " Give yourself no alarm," said an old Genevese, who had come to Divonne to be cured of sleep-
lessness. " He will talk some day when nobody expects it, and speak all three of his languages together.

I had a friend in Berne who had just such a little boy. This poor little devil had an English mother, a French nurse, and heard German all around him. He thought he was in the Tower of Babel, I suppose, for he never said a word till he was four years old. His father feared that he was dumb, and got all the doctors in Berne to give their opinions on him. The doctors physicked him, and nearly pulled his tongue out to see why it never talked; but he made no greater progress for all that. Well, one day, when they had nearly given up all hope of his ever speaking, he came out on a sudden with a whole sentence in English. From that day he talked all his languages, and talked them fluently, just like any other child of four years old. And so it will be with this little chap—never fear."

Strange as it may seem for a Republican to say so, I soon found that I had more national sympathies with these Russians than with any other people that I had met in Europe. As we Americans complain of being traduced and unmeritedly ridiculed by foreign travelers, so had the indignation of these Muscovites been aroused by a series of French Trollopes and German Basil Halls. The Germans indeed, they said, were usually careful observers and conscientious narrators, but the Frenchmen were, almost without exception, superficial, flippant, impertinent, and false. They remarked with some bitterness on the insolent civilization of Western Europe, which would acknowledge no merit, no greatness out of its own geographical boundaries. Like us, too, they relied on the future for making their character known and their claims to respectability acknowledged. "You and we," said they, "have the time to come; we can afford to bear with these people for a season."

Another subject, not so bright in its future aspects, on which we could talk in sympathy, was slavery. As their father owned nineteen hundred serfs, I was rather surprised to find them theoretically abolitionists. But, like the mass of our Northern people, they looked upon emancipation rather as a desideratum than a near expectancy. "Our Nicholas," said Prince Georges, "has declared that he will abolish serfage, but he never will do it, for he never will dare. The question is too tremendous to be solved suddenly, even by despotic power. The wrong will, I am afraid, live on until it is righted by revolution and carnage. My God! if we had only four millions of serfs, like you, we would soon put an end to the system. But just imagine the awful number of fifty millions!"

"Are there any socialistic ideas among the serfs?" I asked—"any thoughts of striking for their liberty?"

"None whatever. They are too ignorant to devise such an abstract idea as the equal rights of man. They are perfectly contented, perfectly tranquil."

"Oh, they love their masters," struck in his wife.

"Love them!" said the prince, laughing. "Ah! that is a good joke. I confess, however, that they do not hate them."

"But they do love them sometimes, Georges," persisted the pretty woman. "There is my maid; she shows that she loves me; and then she tells me that she does."

"My dear wife," said the prince, "she would not

dare to tell you the contrary. You would not give her any more old dresses.

"No," he continued, turning to me, "I do not apprehend an insurrection from any discontent that now exists among our serfs, but I do when I look at the subject as a prophet, from the stand-point of history and of abstract right. It is not natural that a man should always suffer himself to be bought and sold by another man. If one generation does not discover that there is an injustice in this, its sons or its grandsons will.

"But we have one advantage over you Americans. Our slavery is vaster than yours, but not so brutal. We do not separate families. We do not put a serf up at auction, like a horse. We never tear one of our peasants from his native village near Moscow to sell him to some farmer in Kamtschatka. Why do you not begin your work, your inevitable duty, by prohibiting the internal slave-trade?"

"We can not," I confessed. "The owners will not permit it."

"Ah! so even your confident republic has its impossibilities."

One thing particularly surprised me in the conversation of these men, and that was a tendency toward Republican sentiments. They would have laughed at the idea of introducing Republicanism into Russia now; but I am sure that they regarded democracy as the end and right of a highly enlightened people. I suspected them even of being dissatisfied with the present unlimited nature of the imperial authority, although it may be that I misunderstood their very cautious expressions of opinion on this subject. In order to comprehend such a feeling in a Russian noble, it must be noted that the power and dignity of his class have diminished just in proportion to the increased prerogative of the czarship. It is in the position of the English aristocracy before Magna Charta: its greatest antagonist is not the people, but the monarch. The emperor holds it all the more easily in submission because primogeniture is not allowed in Russia, so that the noble families can rarely increase, or even hold for a long time, their wealth and territory. All the sons, be they a dozen, inherit the title and their portion of the property of the father; and thus Russia is full of poor aristocrats, most of whom are dependent upon the civil and military offices for support, and are, consequently, humble servants of his place-dispensing majesty. Then there are the new nobles, mostly rich tradesmen and bankers, who have been elevated by the imperial hand, and are, of course, ready to lick it at the first signal. But the order feels its own degradation, and nourishes within its breast the only enemies whom the Czar has to fear.

Prince Georges talked, in a laughing way, about his ultra-Republican sentiments of boyish days. "I was in a military school; and we children all read Plutarch, and raved about Timoleon and the two Brutuses. Sometimes we made resolutions that, when the emperor next came to visit us, we would treat him with the coolness that such a Tarquin, such a Dionysius deserved. Well, the day came, and the emperor appeared — a tall, magnificent man; how we admired him, notwithstanding our Radicalism! Still, for a moment, there would be a silence. But when the emperor put his hands on one boy's head, and caught up another and kissed him, there was no resisting it. We all burst into a hurrah, and tumbled over each other to get near him, and share in his fondlings and benedictions."

CHAPTER XIV.

STORY-TELLING IN DIVONNE.

PRINCE GEORGES sometimes amused us with stories of his travels, for his nomadic performances by far outpassed those of any other member of our circle. For instance, he had accomplished the gigantic journey from Moscow to Kamtschatka and back by land ; visiting the Polar Asiatic Sea, living under tents of sealskin on the snow, and sledging for hundreds of miles after harnessed dogs. The doctor and his brother narrated their semi-martial experiences in Algeria, while I occasionally told the wonders of Syria, Greece, Constantinople, and Connecticut.

One evening a series of ghost-stories arose from their graves in our memories, and walked slowly down a long, awful passage of the conversation. "It was in Berlin that I became witness of some mysterious circumstances," said Prince Eugene. "I arrived there with only one servant, expecting to be followed in a few days by my family. My first business was to secure a spacious suite of rooms, consisting, in fact, of the two upper stories of a large building. The attic, however, was not only vacant, but unfurnished ; and I took it simply to keep other people out, as the floor below was quite enough for my purpose. I moved in immediately, and passed a few days there without other society than that of my servant. Nothing unusual occurred until evening, when the flow of people and vehicles died away, and the street in front of the house became quiet. Then I was surprised by hearing strange noises in the building, various in sound, though generally resembling muffled peals of laughter; but what struck me as most singular about them was that they seemed to come from the upper story, which I knew to be a desert unfurnished with inhabitants. After listening half an hour, trying to persuade myself that my ears deceived me, I sent my valet up stairs to search out the cause of this curious uproar. He went, and returned saying that the attic was not only perfectly vacant, but perfectly silent. The disturbance, however, still continued, becoming, as evening advanced, louder, clearer, and more continuous. Long peals of laughter, indistinct words, a strange rolling noise, sometimes a sharp clash, and then new bursts of laughter, succeeded each other, until, between perplexed curiosity and nervousness, I got out of all patience. I accused my valet of having been afraid to examine the floor thoroughly, and declared that he must have left some windows open, through which people entered from the adjoining houses. Taking a light, I went up myself; but when I reached the attic the noises had ceased. There was not a person, not a mouse even, not a window ajar, not a trap-door loose, nothing but dusty floors and utter silence. I came down very much perplexed, and almost got into a rage at hearing the clamor recommence the moment I reached the rooms below. I repeated the examination immediately, and several times afterward during the evening, now stealing up softly in the dark, now rushing up with my candle, always thinking that I should catch somebody who had made an almost impossible escape before.   But I constantly had the same ill luck, and finally went to bed, tired out with these chases after sounds without bodies.   I noticed as a very singular circumstance that the noises diminished toward eleven o'clock, and by midnight had ceased entirely.

"The next evening repeated the comedy, with the same incomprehensible rolling, crashing, and laughter ; the same series of garret inquisitions, and the same absurd disappointments.   On the third day I sent for the owner of the house, for the affair was getting to be a serious annoyance.   He looked incredulity when I told my tale ; but I requested him to come and hear for himself that evening.   At eight o'clock he was in my parlor, listening with as much perplexity as I to the rising flow of mysterious noises.   He searched every room and closet, made various rapid forays up stairs, in hopes of surprising some dexterous joker, but descended each time with a face of increased stupefaction.   ' It is perfectly unaccountable,' said he ; ' I have never believed in haunted houses, but this seems very much like one.   If you wish it, I am ready to take back the rooms and release you from your bargain.'

"I was puzzled what to do, for I felt ashamed to quit the house on the ground of ghosts, and yet these disturbances deprived me of all quiet in it.   Suddenly my landlord rose and went to a door, which opened upon a narrow stairway leading to the story below. The passage was no longer used, and the door fastened, but he contrived to open it.   In a moment the mystery was explained: the noises rushed *up* the stairway in a volume. There was a beer-room and a billiard-table below; it was the billiard-balls which I had heard crash and roll; it was the players and beer-drinkers whom I had heard talk and laugh. But, in consequence of some remarkable acoustic peculiarity in the building, all these sounds, the moment that the door was shut, seemed to come from above. If that stairway had not been thought of, I should have been perplexed all my life by a spectral mystery, while the house would probably have acquired a bad name, or even been deserted as a haunted edifice."

"Exactly," said the doctor; "it is very probable. Well, I know a story to the same effect, although not so good a one by a degree. The incidents occurred to my father, who, as I have told you, was a surgeon in Napoleon's army, and held on firm to him down to Waterloo. At the second restoration he lost his commission, retired into the country, and set up for what practice he could find. Well, he contrived to get a wife, and a house to keep her in, or, rather, part of a house, for one half of it was occupied by a good citizen who held a corporalship in the National Guard. The building was divided from front to rear by a long passage; my father occupied the lodgment on one side of it, and the corporal occupied on the other. It was a rambling, eccentric edifice, with its rooms lying about at loose ends, like a crazy man's ideas. The servant-girl's room, for example, was at the back end of this passage, a long distance from the rest of the family, and next door to being out of doors. Now Jeannette, being a mere peasant and unable to read, believed in ghosts of a necessity, and was a little timid about sleeping in such a solitude. But nothing happened to her till a certain winter night, when there was a trifle of snow on the ground, and the winds were blowing like trumpeters. At some late hour she woke up in a fright, with the idea that something or somebody was scratching at her window. The sound had ceased before she quite got her senses, and although she stared hard at the glass she could see nothing. Presently she heard the scratching again; there was no possible mistake about it this time; it continued a little while, and then stopped—mysteriously. It was too modest a noise for a robber, and must necessarily be the work of some ghost who was trying to force an entrance. It was awful; it made the goose-flesh come; it made her hair stand on tiptoe. Imagine, ladies and gentlemen, the horrible circumstances of the situation: a small chamber, at the end of a long passage, at midnight, with something scratching on the window! Can you wonder that my father's unsophisticated servant-maid drew her head under the bed-clothes, and nearly had a nervous crisis? At last came a low, shrill cry, very much, I suppose, like the squeak of a ghost trying to crowd himself through a crack in a window-pane. Gathering all her strength into one sublime effort for safety, Jeannette leaped out of bed, burst open the door, ran along the passage, and fell with a scream just outside of my father's bedroom. My mother started up at the noise, and awoke my father. 'What is the matter?' he grumbled.

"'That scream!' said my mother. 'Didst thou hear it?'

" ' No; where was it ?'

" ' In the hall. It was perfectly horrible. Is it possible that thou didst not hear it ?'

" ' No,' said my father, again; ' but I will go and see if any thing has happened.'

" He got up, stepped into the passage, and of course stumbled over a half dead chambermaid. Taking her into the bed-room, he applied hydropathy, that is to say, threw a tumbler of cold water in her face, and brought her to her senses. As soon as she could speak she told her story, thereby horribly frightening my mother, who, you must know, had not served under Napoleon. ' Ghost!' said my father; ' go to the devil! What are you talking about ? It is a thief, if it is any thing.'

" He took down the old sabre with which he had amputated heads under Napoleon, seized a candle, and set off for the chamber of mysterious scratchings. My mother caught hold of his shirt, declaring that she would not stay alone ; and Jeannette, equally gregarious, staggered after them both, holding fast to my mother's nightgown. In the passage they came upon the corporal of the National Guard, who had slid óut of his room in deshabille to discover the cause of the screaming. My father explained the affair in a wink ; and the corporal, catching down his musket, joined the forlorn hope. His wife said that she would not remain there alone, and, grasping his linen, tagged after him, so that, in fine, the whole five trooped down the cold passage in their shifts. The costume was not exactly that of court ; but then time pressed, and the occasion was grave. At the door of the terrible chamber the women stopped, while the men charged in with arms presented. Nothing was to be seen, so they halted and listened. Presently every one heard distinctly a faint scratching on the window. My father raised it cautiously, while the corporal stood ready to fire, when in jumped the cat. Yes, ladies and gentlemen, the old black cat——ha! ha! ha! The old cat had got out in a cold winter night, and very naturally wanted to get in again——ho! ho! ho!"

Another story which I heard at Divonne was not only curious and mysterious, but rang eloquently on the ear with a jingling of filthy lucre. The count, Trocon, and I sat in the billiard-room, talking over Californian expeditions and specie-huntings of various species.

"If I wanted money, I would go to California," said the count, with a sparkle of golden desire in his eye.

"Ho!" responded Trocon, with a mysterious chuckle, rising and turning his back to the fire. "There are treasures in France, too, which could be had for the digging."

"What do you mean?" asked the count, throwing up his head as if scenting a placer.

"I know what I mean, but it is a secret," replied Trocon, digging his hands resolutely into his pockets.

The count looked perplexed, and so did Trocon; the one fidgeted on his chair, and the other on his feet; the one was anxious to know, and the other equally anxious to tell. There was a brief silence, at the end of which Trocon resumed his seat, leaned forward, and said, in a reduced voice, "Will you promise never to speak of it without my permission?"

"But yes, but certainly," asseverated the count, laying his hands on his knees solemnly, as if he were placing them on an altar.

"But certainly," echoed I.

"Eh! well," continued Trocon, "you know my city, Mantry? It lies about ten leagues from here, on the diligence-route between Geneva and Paris. You traversed it, perhaps, in coming to Divonne?"

"Without doubt, certainly," said the count.

"Certainly," repeated I.

"Eh! well, not quite a league from the city there is a great convent, *very* ancient, on a hill close by a fine forest. This convent is deserted now, because the monks were chased out of France in 1793, and the government seized the property. The government has it still, but the land lies waste, and there is nobody in the building except a keeper, who cultivates the old garden. Eh! well, about five years ago a poor man in our town, who has done a devilish bad business in life, showed me a letter written from America by a monk, who said he was the last of that brotherhood. The letter declared that there was a treasure buried in an iron chest in one corner of the inclosure, under the foundation of a stairway which has been leveled."

"What was the treasure?" asked the count, in a tone as secret as if he was locked inside of a money-safe.

"All the convent plate, and all the money that the brotherhood had when it was dispersed."

"Why didn't this monk come for the treasure himself?" the count continued, as a slight shade of painful doubt crossed his visage

"Perhaps he was afraid," replied Trocon; "but he said in the letter that he was old—too old to enjoy so much money, if he could get it; but he thought it was a pity good silver should be lost, and he wanted his ancient friend to benefit by it. Eh! well, gentlemen, I have held this letter in my own hands. The man who received it wanted me to help find the money, and go shares with him. He thought of climbing the wall by night, and digging; but one night might not have sufficed for that trick, and then he would have paid with his skin if he had been caught at it, for, as I tell you, the land is government property."

"How much would the convent cost?" asked the count, with speculation in his eyes. "Not more than twenty or twenty-five thousand francs, I suppose."

"No, not more; but this poor fellow could not raise the quarter of that."

"But why not interest other people in the project, and take half, if he could not have the whole?"

"Exactly; that was what he wanted to do; but he never dared go to rich men, for fear they would take the whole affair out of his hands, and leave him nothing. He came to people like me, and we naturally hesitated to invest our small capitals in an old convent at the word of a letter. It would have been ruinous to buy and not find a treasure; worse than that, it would have been ridiculous. So the affair went on, until, in fine, I nearly forgot it. It is now two or three years, perhaps more, since I have heard speak of the convent treasure."

The count was evidently somewhat fascinated by the romantic bubble which had been blown for him. He wondered how large the treasure might be, and observed that it would be a pious action to restore it, or even *part* of it, to the Church. He put a variety of questions to Trocon concerning the situation and quality of the building, the possibility of changing it into a water-cure establishment, the value of its lands for agricultural purposes, and the supposed price set upon the whole demesne by government. The other promised to obtain him all needful information to commence the enterprise; he would guide him to the convent, show him the metalliferous spot, and get him a sight of the letter.

"Good," said the count. "We will go there together some day, after we have finished our cures. By the way, it would be well to obtain the services of a mesmeric medium. I have an immense confidence in mesmerism; I have known some cases of the most extraordinary. I will look up a subject in Paris, and see what he can reveal. You will come to see me at my rooms in the Faubourg St. Germain. If you can not come, write where you will meet me; we will go to the spot in company."

There the matter rested. The count left, and we heard no news from him except that he was in Paris, and well. Very likely he had lost his interest in the gilded mystery. Three weeks or more after his departure, the conversation at table happened to float into the confused eddies of a discussion concerning mesmerism. "I can relate a rather curious circumstance connected with that subject," said the doctor. "I was driving in my calèche near Mantry, about two years ago, when I overtook a woman walking alone. She was a decent-looking person of about thirty, and I invited her to take a seat beside me. She accepted, mounted, talked away heartily, and soon managed to give me a pretty full account of herself. She said that she and her husband were public officials, after a fashion, having been hired to take care of a deserted convent about a league from Mantry, which was government property. She added that there had been reports of a treasure hidden somewhere in the precincts, but that no attempt had been made to discover it until a few nights before our meeting. They were then awakened after midnight by noises about the building, and heard them continue some time, but dared not go out to discover the cause of them for fear of being attacked by robbers. The next morning they found a deep excavation freshly made under the foundations of a ruined stairway in one corner of the inclosure. During the day her husband went down to the city on some errand, and mentioned to his acquaintances the fright that he had just experienced. In exchange, he learned that a gentleman from Lyons, accompanied by a well-known mesmeric medium, had visited Mantry, with the supposed intention of discovering the convent treasure; that they had been absent from the hotel all the night previous, and had returned to it in the morning only to take a private carriage and set out immediately on the road to Lyons. That was all that any one knew certainly, but the woman fully believed that these people had carried off the treasure. It was a curious story."

G

While the doctor was thus narrating, I saw that Trocon listened in anxious silence. "My God!" he broke out at the conclusion, "there goes the count's money."

CHAPTER XV.

MESMERISM IN DIVONNE.

ONE of the peculiarities of us hydropaths at Divonne, at least while I remained, was to talk a great deal about animal magnetism. The fanaticism of table-turnings, indeed, had not yet reached France, so that we attempted no waltzes with the doctor's mahogany, and used our hats only to hang on nails or to cover our craniums. Still, wonders were enacted among us, and there were so many other wonders told of, that I have been able to fill a whole chapter with somnambulism, mesmerism, and their sister mysteries. Refreshing be the slumber into which it lulls thee, O reader!

Among our patients was a jolly, kindly, talkative man called Robson, or some such name, a native of the north of Ireland, but very Scotchy in his accent, as well as in his high cheek-bones, sandy hair, and dry, red complexion. Trocon hated him because he was an Englishman, and believed, without the slightest provocation, that he abused his sick wife; for it is a matter of faith with common Frenchmen that all John Bulls are abominable, shameless Bluebeards; that they beat their better halves, put halters around their necks, and sell them for a shilling apiece.

One day, after dinner, we were all gathered in the parlor, talking as sensibly as we could talk on such an absurd subject as mesmerism, when Robson produced from his pocket a zinc button with a bit of copper let into the centre of one of its faces, and declared that by means of this magic circlet he could magnetize any person at all susceptible to magnetic influences. Advancing with a bow and a smile to the wife of Prince Georges L——, he said, "Madame, I think you would be an excellent subject; will you allow me to experiment on you?"

The princess started from her chair as if he had offered to bite her, and retreated several steps, murmuring excitedly, "No, no, I have a horror of mesmerism."

As Robson seemed slightly mortified by this repulse, my socialistic friend Jolivet politely stepped forward and offered to undergo the trial. The Irishman surveyed his cool, philosophical visage somewhat dubiously, but accepted the challenge with a proud confidence in the metal of his button. He made Jolivet sit down, put the bit of zinc in the palm of his right hand, and directed him to fix his eyes steadily on the glittering yellow spot in the centre. The whole company gathered round with a mingled interest of fun and curiosity. Doctor Vidart showed his small white teeth, and glanced alternately from his countryman to *perfide Albion*, evidently wondering what gull or canard was to be hatched now. The Princess Georges L—— watched with real alarm the intentness of Jolivet's gaze, and drew nervously away from him, as if she feared to find herself within the circle of some mysterious fascination. Her husband leaned against a pillar, crossed his grenadier arms on his large chest,

and looked on as absorbedly as if he were studying
his favorite author, the political economist Bastiat.
Robson stood by his victim, regarding him attentively, agitated but confident. At the end of five minutes
or so he seemed to think that his magic had worked
effectually. Removing the button with anxious cau-
tiousness, so as not to break the spell, he proceeded to
draw his fingers over Jolivet's eyes in such a manner
as to close them, followed this up with a few passes,
and then shouted, in a voice of necromantic command,
" *Vous ne pouvez pas ouvrir vos yeux*" (You can not
open your eyes).

Jolivet made, to all appearance, a neck-breaking
effort; his eyelids quivered, and, so to speak, stood
ajar.

" You can not," vociferated Robson; " no, you
can not; I tell you you can not—you can not open
them."

The little lean man worked like a thrashing machine;
his arms flew, and the potent passes fell in swift succession; he grew scarlet in the face, and capered as
if he were performing a scalp-dance. Jolivet appeared
to sink, in spite of himself, under the supernatural influence; his eyelashes drooped again, and his head
fell back like the nerveless head of a swooning man.

" He is one of the best subjects that I ever saw; I
never magnetized any one so easily before," gasped
Robson, in a perspiration, as he prepared for another
trial of his power. He made some fresh passes down
the arms, the body, and the legs of his captive.
" Now you can not get up," he exclaimed; " no, you
can not—you can not stir. I tell you that you can

not stir. You are my prisoner. You can not move hand nor foot."

All this he rattled off with astonishing vehemence, in an accent that came from at least as far as the north of Ireland, pawing, sputtering, and dancing about like an angry cat, his face as flushed and fiery as that of a pumpkin jack-o'-lantern. Jolivet put forth his whole strength to rise; his arms and legs moved almost convulsively; he very nearly attained a staggering equilibrium, but the pitiless passes rained upon him like a shower of brickbats, and vanquished, exhausted, he sank slowly back into a lethargic movelessness. Robson, not a little tired himself, wiped his forehead and looked around with an air of triumph. "Ladies and gentlemen," said he, "I have subjected this man's physique to my will. I shall now subject his intellect, or at least his imagination, to it."

Turning to his victim, he gave him permission to rise, and at once, as if relieved of a mighty weight, Jolivet resumed his perpendicular. "Why, you are out of doors," continued Robson, in a bamboozling tone, very much as nurses talk to children. "Do you not see that we are out of doors?"

Jolivet nodded cheerfully, as if pleasantly conscious of his extra-mural condition.

"Yes, you are out of doors, in a beautiful garden," proceeded the humbugging Irishman. "What a beautiful garden this is all around you!"

Jolivet looked at the tables, the chairs, and the carpetless floor with an aspect of horticultural admiration.

"Why do you not pick some of these lovely flowers

at your feet?" inquired Robson, as seductive as Satan in Paradise. "You need not be afraid. I give you liberty to do so. Pick a fine bouquet for one of the ladies."

The Frenchman stooped, and began to gather imaginary posies with an air of infantine delight.

"Stop, my friend," called the necromancer. "Do you not see that elegant butterfly, with gold wings? Catch it—run after it—quick, before it is too high!"

Away went Jolivet down the saloon, knocking the chairs right and left, and jumping over the sofas in an uproarious steeple-chase after the fabulous insect.

"There, you have caught it," interposed Robson. "Now bring it here, and show it to the ladies," he added, with true Irish gallantry. Back trotted Jolivet, breathless, but with a smirk of babyish delight on his philosophical phiz as he carefully handled the assumed prize, and made the motions of showing it around the company. There was by this time a great sensation. The doctor's skeptical smile had changed to an expression of curiosity and grave professional interest. Prince Georges had started from his pillar, and was talking rapidly with his brother in Russian. His wife had retreated to the other end of the room, and thrown herself on a sofa, covering her face with her white fingers. "Oh, I am frightened," she said, when I asked her what was the matter. "It is shocking to see one man so completely under the influence of another. It is insanity, and perhaps worse. Oh, but I have known such horrible things of magnetism! I will tell you them some time."

The next thing that started up Jolivet was a bear,

which made him dodge about the saloon in a state of intense terror, until Robson was kind enough to call the animal off.   But now came the explanation of these mysteries, the disentanglement of this supernatural drama.   As the Frenchman passed me in one of his desperate doubles to avoid the fictitious Bruin, a faint smile on his mouth broadened to a grin, and he whispered rapidly, " Do you understand ?"

It was all a trick, then—a hoax of Jolivet's on *perfide Albion!*   Yet even now, so admirable was his acting that I could scarcely believe in the jest, and wondered whether, after all, he were not really magnetized without being conscious of it.   Still, I whispered the joke to some of the others, and quiet grins of comprehension began to steal from visage to visage.   Robson, in the mean time, saw nothing, suspected nothing; he sent the solemn jester on one wild goose chase after another ; he shouted himself hoarse with commands, as his subject sometimes got fractious and refused to obey ; in short, for more than half an hour he kept Jolivet and himself in a perspiration, and us in smothered laughter.   Once in a while, when by chance he detected a smile on the Frenchman's face, he made new passes at him to bring him back, as he said, to a state of perfect somnolency.   At last, after they were both tired out, he willed his subject to sit, and removed the magnetic influence, in the most scientific manner, by a series of reversed passes.   It was wonderful to see how naturally Jolivet came to, how dreamingly he opened his eyes, how he rubbed and stretched himself, and what difficulty he had in discovering where he was.   Every body was satisfied with him, and none more so than the stultified Irishman. We waited with many sidelong smiles until Robson left the room, and then we poured congratulations of laughter on our admirable comedian.

" But you deceived all of us," said Prince Georges ; " that poor man was not your only victim."

" And was it all pretense, Monsieur Jolivet ?" asked his princess. " Did you feel nothing all the time that you were doing all those things ?"

" Nothing, Madame, except, indeed, a slight blindness or dizziness at first, produced, I suppose, by looking so long at one object."

" And so there is no power in the button ?"

" None at all. It is an absurdity. The idea of any power in it is ridiculous."

We kept the joke a secret from Robson, and had more fun in the evening. Trocon was magnetized then, and put the saloon into confusion with his outrageous struggles to escape the Irishman's bulls and bears, or to overtake his butterflies. We laughed ourselves tired ; laughed till the jest began to seem stale, flat, and unprofitable ; but, laugh as we might, the infatuated Robson suspected no deceit. The next day, that Anglophobian Trocon flatly told him of the hoax, and made it a matter of much public stentorian merriment. Even yet the man would believe nothing ; even yet he put faith in the wonders that his button had seemed to work ; and he turned away from Trocon's mocking tale with contemptuous, angry incredulity.

" They may giggle as much as they like," he said to me, " but they are mistaken. That man was really magnetized ; but, you see, the sleep was imperfect ; he partially remembers what he did, and he thinks, consequently, that he was not in a state of somnolency; but I know better.   I know that he was not perfectly himself.   Don't you think so, now?"

I hemmed and hahed a kind of assent; a hypocritical policy, indeed, but still a charitable one, for it was certainly kindest to break the man's misfortune to him little by little.   Jolivet's position was, for some days, a delicate one; but he manœuvred himself out of it with a dexterity worthy of Beaumarchais or Talleyrand, parrying the Irishman's angry queries and eluding his accusations with a most deceptive mixture of evasions and retractions.

"Monsieur," Robson would begin, "do you mean to assert that you were not really magnetized the other day?"

"Eh! well, it is difficult to say; I had some very peculiar sensations."

"Ah!" said Robson, with a look of triumph at me; "you had a sensation of dizziness, perhaps—a rather confused sensation?"

"Yes, especially when I got among the chairs and tables."

"I mean," answered Robson, growing indignant again, "I mean a confusion of mind.   You could not exactly tell whether you were awake or dreaming."

"Eh! well, yes; it was something like a dream, I must acknowledge."

"Exactly.   But now, when people dream, they are asleep, you know; so you must have been asleep.   Was it not so?"

"No—no—I—I—rather think that I was not precisely asleep."

"How, sir! do you mean to say that you were broad awake at the time that you pretended to be in a magnetic state?"

"Excuse me, I did not say broad awake. There are states during which somnolency and wakefulness verge into one another. I do not like to affirm positively what my condition was. It was a very curious one."

"So you really had some curious sensations? I thought so. Well, what were they, as near as you can describe?"

"Why, it is difficult to state such matters with accuracy. A sensation is so vague, so spiritual a thing that it is impossible for language to precisely grasp and convey it."

"Did you ever have such sensations before, Monsieur Jolivet? I ask you seriously."

"Yes—on the whole, yes, I think I have—somewhat similar, but always under very peculiar circumstances."

"I do believe that that man was really magnetized," said Robson, turning to address me in English. "He doesn't know whether he was or not. This Trocon says that he wasn't, because he thinks it is a pretty joke to say so; but I know better. Mark my words, sir, that man was really asleep."

Gradually, however, he allowed himself to believe; at first, it is true, wrathfully and with much offended dignity, but thinking better of it soon, and falling back into his natural kind sociability.

"I will tell you some things that I know of this animal magnetism," said Princess Georges L—— to me. " You shall judge from them whether I am not right in being afraid of these mesmerizers and their powers. This Monsieur Robson has not magnetized any body; perhaps he can not do it; but there are people who can. I had a cousin who was engaged to a gentleman in Moscow. He was a very successful magnetizer; not by profession, you understand, but for his amusement. He magnetized my cousin often, and, after a time, he brought her so completely under his influence that he could put her asleep in a moment. We begged her not to submit to it, but she was so fascinated by him that she would not hearken to us; and I think that he magnetized her so often in order to subject her perfectly to his will, and thus finally gain possession of her property. At last her friends learned some very bad things of him—oh! very bad; and so they broke off the engagement. He was furious, and declared that he had an empire over her which should give him revenge. Eh! well, he used to walk by the house and magnetize her from the street, so that, no matter what she was doing or with whom she was talking, she would fall asleep immediately. Imagine what a dreadful thing that was, to be so under the influence of this bad and revengeful man. But that was not all. Her mother tried to rescue her from this gentleman's power by taking her to a country seat two hundred leagues from Moscow. But even there he would mesmerize her; yes, without leaving the city or his room, he would will that she should sleep; and then she would fall into this dreadful magnetic state, and remain in it until they brought some mesmerizer to break the charm. He persecuted her in that way for a long time; and he could still, if he desired to do so. That is one affair that has made me so afraid of mesmerism. I know some other things about it, but none so bad as that. I do believe that evil spirits have much to do with it, and that people act very wrongly in meddling with such an awful mystery."

Now, then, for some of the serious mesmeric, magnetic, or somnambulistic phenomena which occurred in Divonne. Two or three weeks before my departure, a sick servant-girl belonging in Geneva came to the Establishment. An excitable, half-hypped creature, she soon began to exhibit nervous crises of a singular character, during which she was able, although confined in bed, to tell what persons were in the passages, and even in the various chambers of the building. For instance, she one day let out the small scandal that the maid of an English lady, who lodged in a different story and at quite a distance, was receiving, in the absence of her mistress, a friendly visit from the valet of Prince Eugene. How she discovered these things, whether by an unnatural and diseased susceptibility of the ear, or whether by some stupid spiritual means of knowledge, is one of those questions that compel me to pause for a reply.

But this damsel's performances in the way of second-sight were mere fiddle-faddle in comparison with the magnetic feats of a lady who was under treatment at the Establishment the year before. She was a resident of Nyon, in the Swiss canton of Vaud; about thirty-five years of age, I think; placed in highly respectable society; married, and in excellent circumstances otherwise. Like the Genevese girl, she had violent

nervous attacks, similar to cataleptic fits, if there be
such a thing as catalepsy. She was easily mesmerized
by the common system of passes; often, too, she fell involuntarily into the magnetic slumber.   It is a permis-
sible eccentricity, I believe, in mesmerized persons, to
show a particular attraction toward some individuals,
and an equally strong repulsion from others, without
giving any reasons for the said sentiments, or following them up in ordinary life.   The high favorite of this lady, during her unnatural sleep, was the
doctor's brother, and her chief abomination, even to
spasms, grimaces, and flight, was the doctor himself.
These feelings were remarkable for the distinctness
and violence of their expression, but still more remarkable because they were almost the converse of her
preferences while awake, when the doctor was her favorite.   It was a strange thing, several persons assured
me, to see this lady moving in her sleep about the
grounds ; meeting one patient with a smile of supreme
pleasure, shuddering and grimacing at the approach of
another, flying from a third, or passing him at the
greatest distance allowed by the breadth of the pathway.   She was so weak as often to be incapable of
walking until she had been mesmerized ; and, as
movement is necessary after the baths, they were
obliged, nearly every day, to throw her into the slumber.   By this constant use, her mesmeric capacities
were developed to an extraordinary degree, and she became one of the most remarkable mediums that I ever
heard mentioned.

For instance, while in a somnambulic state, she was
asked by the doctor's brother what she saw.

" I see my sister-in-law, who lives at Nyon," she answered. "It is strange, too, she is not at Nyon—she
is somewhere else. Ah! I see ; she is in my house
outside of the city ; she is laying down carpets and arranging the rooms for me. That is very kind indeed."

After some moments she spoke again.

" They have brought her a letter, and she is reading it. It is for me."

" What is in the letter ?" asked M. Vidart. " Can
you read it ?"

" No, I can not see it very well. Stop! let me
look a moment. Ah! yes, I can read it now."

. She repeated, as if verbatim, what seemed to be a
short note, referring, I believe, to the furniture of the
country house. M. Vidart took down the words as
they were spoken, made a memorandum of the time,
and immediately dispatched a servant to Nyon, to see
if the vision had been correct. The Nyonese lady
wrote back that she was in the said house at the hour
mentioned ; that she had occupied herself there with
cleaning the rooms and setting the furniture in order ;
and that, receiving a note directed to her sister-in-law,
she had taken the liberty to open it. By the messen-
ger she forwarded the note, which proved to be word
for word what M. Vidart had written down from the
lips of the somnambulist.

But on another occasion this invalid's second-sight
went farther still, and struck, to all appearance, within
the solemn boundaries of the miraculous. In a general way, I entertain very disrespectful opinions of
modern miracles. I can barely manage to suppose
that a magnetic subject may look into a distant pres-

ent; but I know that he can not see the future, for the reason that the future is always unaccomplished and inexistent. Yet this woman certainly uttered a prophecy, which, at the appointed day and hour, had an astonishing, improbable fulfillment. Bound in one of her usual mesmeric slumbers, she began to talk of an approaching nervous crisis, more violent than any she had yet experienced, mentioning the date on which it would occur, even to the hour, which was a little after noontide. It would last eighteen days, she said; she dreaded to look forward to it; still, when it was over, she would be better.

"Do you see no means of averting this attack?" asked M. Vidart.

"No, I see none."

"Will it be caused by any particular circumstance?"

"Yes; it will follow upon a great fright that is going to befall me."

"Is there no way of avoiding this fright?"

"No, I see none. No, there is none."

"What will be the cause of this fright?"

"I can not see."

"Search carefully."

"I do so; I am watching; but no, I can not see. It wearies me to look."

On waking, she, as usual, had no recollection of what had passed in her sleep; and, by the doctor's orders, every one kept silence on the subject, lest the mere expectation of such an attack should produce it; so that when the day came she knew nothing of her prophecy. A constant watch was maintained over her; and, on various pretenses, she was kept in her chamber, her husband remaining with her most of the time, and guarding vigilantly against every possible cause of terror.   During the forenoon of the day predicted, he received a visit from an old friend, who had stopped at Divonne expressly to see him, and who proposed that they should take a jovial dinner together at the village tavern.   He declined, alleging that his wife was more unwell than usual, and that he thought it imprudent to leave her.   "But stay thou and dine with me," he added; "we will make a party of three in my wife's room."

The other accepted, and at one they sat down to table.   The meal was about half over, when the guest fell out of his chair in an apoplectic fit, and expired almost immediately.   The sick woman burst into hysterics of terror, lapsing at length into a cataleptic state, in which for eighteen days she remained rigid and senseless.   Furthermore, in order that the prophecy might be fulfilled in every particular, a considerable improvement in her health dated from the close of this frightful paralysis.

Now I can not explain this extraordinary circumstance in accordance with any known law of nature, but I think I can affirm positively that it happened.   I know that the brothers Vidart are credible men; that this event was a common matter of talk among the patients of the Establishment; and that the doctor has boldly published an account of it in a Report on his first two years of hydropathic treatment.   I have not that Report with me, and it is possible that my memory has varied from it in some particulars; but I think that, at all events, I have not exaggerated the marvelous-

ness of the story.   I can give no explanation, and I
suppose that I might as well not trouble myself to
ask one.   Reichenbach is probably the only notable
man of science who would try to answer me, and
Reichenbach is hidden at Schloss Reisenberg, near Vienna, making magnetic experiments in the most occult
of dark chambers.

But I must come to an end in my gossip about Divonne.   The first of June arrived before I quitted this
French hamlet, where I had passed nearly eight
months in a damp but most agreeable manner.   My
recovery, if not complete, had at least reached a point
far beyond the hopes of a year previous.   Given up
as a bad job by a dozen allopaths in succession, I had
been raised by the chill potency of pure water to as
high a degree of health as is the ordinary award of
mortals.   It was time to see Paris and Italy again—
time to walk anew beneath the glory of pictures and
the grandeur of temples.   I bade a truly reluctant
adieu to my friends of all nations, English, French,
Swiss, and Russians.   The brothers Vidart kissed me
on both cheeks, and on both cheeks I kissed them in
reply.   We tore our amicable mustaches apart, and
I found myself once more alone in Europe.

CHAPTER XVI.

A CHEAP WATERING-PLACE.

SHOULD one of my readers desire to pass a cheap summer in a picturesque locality, I can tell him where he may realize his wishes. In the green valley of the Rhone, a few miles above the head of Lake Leman, and nearly surrounded by mountains, lies a little Swiss village called Bex, somewhat celebrated for its salt and medicinal springs. As its diurnal board and lodging only cost two francs and a half, and the style of entertainment is proportionably simple, the idlers and invalids who fill its brace of hotels are usually persons of moderate fortunes and unostentatious habits. I was impelled to Bex by economical motives, for one letter of credit was nearly exhausted, and its successor did not arrive as I had expected.

From Geneva a nice little steam-boat carried me at a very respectable speed up the clear length of Leman. Green mountains, snowy mountains, rose all along the eastern horizon in a wonderful waste of wild, various magnificence, below which sloped down to the lake grassy shores, waving with trees, flecked with country seats and farm-houses, or more densely populous here and there with villages and quaint little cities. On the other side, beneath the great mass of the Jura, I could see the hill of Divonne and many other landmarks familiar to my footsteps. I passed Nyon, helmeted with its old chateau, and strained my eyes use-

lessly to catch sight of Maître Jacques on his pedestal in the market-street.   Vevay welcomed me for the
night to the hospitality of one of its clean and elegant
hotels.

In the morning I met what was novel to me, an
American.   I was fast asleep when the news of his
presence in Vevay was thundered at my door by the
knuckles of a heralding waiter.   At my invitation to
enter, the rapping individual respectfully glided into
the room, and announced that General Jones was in
the parlor, and would be happy to see me.

"You are mistaken," said I, rubbing my eyes
open.

"Excuse me, Monsieur; not at all; he is really
there."

"I mean that *he* is mistaken," I replied, gradually
getting my senses together.

"It is possible," said the waiter, dubiously.

"I think that he wants somebody else," resumed I,
beginning to define my position more exactly.   "I
believe I don't know any General Jones."

"Monsieur calls himself Monsieur De Forest—is it
not so?"

"Exactly."

"Eh! well, it is precisely Monsieur De Forest that
General Jones demands to see."

"Indeed!   Perhaps he knows some of my family.
Perhaps he wants to lend me some money now.   Is
he an American or an Englishman?"

"An American, Monsieur; from the United States
even."

"Tell him that I will be down directly."

"Yes, Monsieur."

The waiter disappeared, and, dressing hastily, I hurried down stairs to the cozy little breakfast-hall, which also served as a reception-room. It was empty ; but presently a small, soft-footed, smiling gentleman of sixty-five stepped gently into it through a door which opened on the garden. A careful look at his quiet little figure and benevolent face satisfied me that we had never met before. Now, thinks I to myself, you are going to apologize ; now you are going to blame yourself severely for your mistake ; now you are going to say how sorry you are for having called me up at seven in the morning. Not at all. He smiled his way toward me, bowed with cheerful politeness, and said, in a low, pleasant voice, " Mr. De Forest, I believe."

I inclined and smiled, for his courtesy was irresistible, and would have mollified a John Bull, had it been even three o'clock in the morning.

"My name is Jones, sir—General Jones, of Baltimore."

I bowed again, shook hands with him, and waited for further developments.

"I saw your name on the book, sir."

"Indeed ! ah !"

"I saw that you were an American," he finished, with the same smile of unspeakable good-nature.

That was it. He had seen that I was an American. That was the reason why he called me up at seven in the morning. That was the reason why he wanted to get a sight of my unknown physiognomy. I saw his character at a glance, and the style of man to which he belonged. He was one of that large class of excellent

citizens and bad cosmopolites who divide humanity
into two species, foreigners and Americans; the former
a queer and incomprehensible set at best, the latter one
huge brotherhood of fine fellows, who can never know
too much of each other.

"I took the liberty of calling you up, sir, thinking
you might be going to Berne," he continued. "I am
going to Berne myself, sir; but, unfortunately, I have
lost my company. I can not bear to travel alone. I
do not enjoy myself, sir, unless I have some American
along with me. I have been traveling with young
Mr. Smith, of New York, sir, of the firm of Smith &
Company—a fine young man, sir, a very fine young
man. Do you know Mr. Smith? No? I should be
happy to introduce you, sir. You would be pleased
to know him. One of the finest young Americans
that I ever saw, sir. It does my heart good, sir, to
meet these young fellows about Europe who are an
honor to their country."

Thus he ran on in an amiable, smiling, garrulous
style, through which his patriotism shone like a sun
through a genial noontide. I told him that, unfortunately, I was not going to Berne, but that we could at
least breakfast together before he departed. At table
I happened to mention that he was the first American
to whom I had spoken for nine months or over. He
fell back in his chair with amazement, and then, laying down his knife and fork, said, in a tone of mild
reproach, "Sir, you must not forget your language
and your country."

From his conversation I found that he was a man
of excellent social position, and knew personally many

of our leading characters at Washington. We parted on rising from the breakfast-table, and never met afterward.

With due respect to the opinion of General Jones, who is an older and more noticeable person than myself, I think it is folly to consort much abroad with Americans. It is pleasant, indeed, to follow out such a patriotic line of conduct; but, on the other hand, foreign languages are not acquired, foreign character is not effectively studied, and the tourist returns home with very nearly the same set of ideas that he possessed at starting. Now all wisdom is surely not confined by American shores, and even religion seems to have existed before the Declaration of Independence. A man may learn something good, therefore, by frequenting the society of Europeans, and, at all events, he is pretty sure to learn something novel. "Englishmen do not travel to see Englishmen," says Sterne, and the maxim might profitably be made universal in its application.

Speaking of American travelers *pur sang*, I may as well mention one of my compatriots whom I saw at Vevay on a subsequent visit. Landing from the steamer in a flat-bottomed boat, I beheld among the trunks and boxes which filled the bow a little withered man of forty-five, remarkable at first sight for a most care-worn expression, as if he were worried nearly to death by constantly looking after his baggage. He wore a black dress coat, black pants, black beaver, and showed a dark face, indigoed in spots by an intensely black beard of two days' growth; in short, he was one of those men who give you the impression of having very little white about them, and of that little being mostly blue.   He held by the hand a dingy youngster, evidently his son, about the size of a twelve-years old boy, but otherwise as soberly venerable in appearance as a Theban mummy.   As soon as the scow touched the shore, both scrambled out in great haste, and began to watch with nervous solicitude the landing of the baggage.   Presently the black-and-blue gentleman, unable to repress his apprehensions, stepped up to one of the porters, and said in English, in an anxious, confidential tone, "Won't you bring that black trunk ashore? That black one—there—at the end of the boat."

"*Comment, Monsieur?*" said the burly, astonished Swiss.

"I don't speak French," remarked my countryman, slowly, distinctly, and with a gravity, a concern which was almost anguish.   "I don't speak French; but I want that black trunk at the end of the boat."

"*Je ne comprends pas, Monsieur.*"

"I say I don't speak French; but it's the black trunk—the black one—*black*—BLACK."

By dint of pointing very hard with his umbrella, he eventually made himself understood.   The distinguished black trunk was safely disembarked and consigned to a baggage-cart, wherepon chip and block trotted off before it to a hotel.

"Mon Dieu, Monsieur," said the chief waiter of the same hotel to me, "what a quantity of your people travel without speaking one word of any language but their own!   They are astonishing for that.   We have English and Germans here sometimes who speak very little French, but they know something of it, or at least have some linguist in the party.   But Americans come here by the half dozen, by the dozen, by twenty together, and not an individual of the whole set can understand the first word that is said to him. It is extraordinary, Monsieur—really comic sometimes."

It *is* comic and extraordinary both. Considering what a practical people we are, our neglect of living languages is marvelous as well as absurd. Of what use are Greek and Latin to the mass of our young people, whether boys or girls, compared with French and German? How many of our valedictorians, after seven years' hard study over the classics, could make a bargain in the tongue of Cicero, or understand a new joke of Aristophanes? I need not dilate upon the facts that Cicero is now beyond the reach of a trade, and that Aristophanes perpetrates no more witticisms. But this is a great subject, and I shall therefore let it slide, as the bear said when he got out of the way of the avalanche.

Instead of describing Clarens and Chillon, I shall refer the insatiable reader to Rousseau, Byron, and a host of other depictive people who have visited these famous places. Taking an economical omnibus at Villeneuve, I proceeded through a delightful verdure, dewy with fresh showers, to Bex. I was installed in a room of about seven feet by nine, walled with pasteboard, or something equally thin, and furnished much in the simple style of Graefenberg. At the *table d'hôte* there were something like thirty persons, of whom more than half were subjects of her Britannic majesty. On my right was an Irish widow, past meridian, but lively, with two blonde daughters of nineteen and twenty, the youngest decidedly handsome. Directly

H

opposite them sat an Irish doctor, a middle-aged man of uncommon jolliness, with one blue eye aslant, and both moistened by *kirschwasser*.   "Madame," said he, dipping a table-spoon into some equivocal hash, "will ye allow me to help ye to some of this dish?   I should be happy to tell ye what it is, but in me ignorance of the French language, and especially of the French cookery-book, the thing is impossible."

Every body around laughed, of course; and as a laugh is an introduction at Bex, our end of the table was soon in a breeze of conversation.   It was not long before I discovered a person who seemed to have some rights of intimacy with my lady neighbors.   I wish to be as far as possible from blabbing a secret, but, as the affair has probably gone much farther before this, there can be no harm in insinuating that he was the engaged lover of the youngest and prettiest of the two Irish sisters.   A very homely fellow he was, to claim so handsome a girl; not less than forty, I am sure, and as stupid a man as ever wore buttons.   I should say that he was stupid so far as my insight extended, for I heard that he was well educated, and could talk on some subjects very sensibly.   Unfortunately, those particular subjects never came up while I had the excitement of being in his company.   He was evidently as bashful as a child, and awkward too in his bashfulness beyond patience.   It was laughable to see him with those lovely girls, and to note the contrast between their young gayety and his elderly embarrassment.   Occasionally he made a clumsy effort to appear easy, and struggled into a broad, unexpected laugh, but inevitably finished by getting frightened and shutting up his mouth all at once, as if he had forgotten why he opened it.

"What a curious fellow!" said a dark, slender, elderly West Indian to me, as this remarkable lover passed the bench where we were enjoying a cool twilight breeze. "Why, he is a monomaniac—nothing less. I have seen him before—met him at Naples. He wouldn't go down stairs the right way, but always backed down, because he had an idea that the other mode of descent injured his digestion. Extraordinary man for that bright girl to take up with. He is rich, they say, and of a very good family. But it's wrong, sir; it's against nature. They'll come to grief."

An equally curious and much more amusing personage was the Irish doctor, whom I soon discovered to be a man of fine capacities and attainments, gifted also with the fluent conversation and abundant humor indigenous to the Emerald Isle. He had an intense dislike to the encumbrance of baggage, and never carried either trunk or carpet-bag. To supply the deficiency, he had got himself an overcoat with pockets a foot and a half deep, in which he stowed a pair of shoes, four shirts, four pair of socks, and a couple or so of handkerchiefs. "It's decidedly more convaynient than a trunk," he observed to me. "Don't ye see? I jist put me overcoat on me arm and walk off, and that's an end of it. I never have any of your foreign porters around me, wanting to carry me trunks; no extra baggage to pay for either, and no trouble at the custom-houses. But it produces a curious effect, I assure ye. When I landed at Boulogne, I took me coat on me arm, and was walking off free and easy to

find a hotel, ye see.   One of the custom-house men
spied me, and says he, '*Monsieur! Monsieur! bagage!*' says he; '*bagage!*'   Well, I jist put me hand
on me coat and nodded, and the fellow grinned, ye see,
and never said another word.   Don't ye see?   At
Meurice's Hotel they always called me the *Monsieur
sans bagage*.   People laugh, of course, but it saves a
deal of trouble.   Now don't ye see?"

The doctor cherished the old English idea that
fighting is an essential part of a boy's education.
"Why, I'll tell ye an anecdote," said he.   "Jist before
I left Ireland, the little son of one of my old friends
came to me—a bright little fellow, that I take as much
delight in as if he was me own.   He told me how another boy had been insulting him.   'Well,' says I,
'an' what did ye do to him?'   Says he, 'I hit him *so*,
right aside of his head.'   'Well,' says I, 'ye did
wrong; ye shouldn't have hit him that way; ye
should have hit him *so*, straight forward from the
shoulder, and right between the eyes.'   That's the
kind of advice that I think is good for boys.   Don't
ye see?"

This reminds me of what I heard from Mrs. L——,
the wife of an English clergyman of genteel birth, who
has a brother in Parliament, and whose father is a
bishop.   Mrs. L—— said that when her husband was
at school, his right reverend parent used to give him
sixpence every time he "whopped" a boy bigger than
himself.   Robust education that, for a family so
much in the apostolic line.   I wonder how much St.
Paul would have given a boy for whopping a schoolfellow?

My most interesting acquaintance at Bex was Monsieur Henri M——, a young man of one of those ancient though untitled families which constitute the noblesse of Berne. That famous canton, it must be noted, was for centuries little more than an oligarchy, ruled by a race of patricians as sternly proud and imperious as the old Claudii or Cornelii of Rome. One of the ancestors of my friend had commanded in the first battle of Novara, fought between the Swiss and the soldiers of Francis I. of France, where nine thousand mountaineer spearmen rushed on the intrenchments of twenty-six thousand trained mercenaries—infantry, artillery, and cavalry—and, after a horrible hand-to-hand carnage, obtained an astonishing victory, killing ten thousand of their enemies on the spot, and so dismaying the rest that they fled altogether from Italy.

The Bernese aristocracy still exist as a separate class, seldom intermarrying with the commonalty of the city. Several of the families, and perhaps most of them, possess a fund, in some cases of considerable amount, which is applied to the support of such representatives of the race as are unable to live in a dignified manner on their own resources. The patrician influence, too, is considerable in providing small offices for decayed gentility, and thus it rarely happens that a sprig of ancient Bernese stock is obliged to dirty itself with any plebeian occupation.

Mr. M—— spoke English, French, and German with equal facility, the former with such an American accent that I at first addressed him as a fellow-countryman. The doctor, therefore, could talk with him, and he took occasion to attack him one day for remaining a bachelor. "Here ye are, Mr. M——," said he, "a man with sense enough to perceive the advantages of matrimony, and yet ye won't put your fingers into the cake to pull out a plum. Have ye any philosophical objections to marriage? Have ye, now?"

"Certainly not. I think that every man ought to marry, unless there should be particular circumstances in his case to render it imprudent or improper."

"Then why don't ye set the example, instead of idling away your life in talking about it? What is the use of making a hypocrite of yourself by discoursing in this Christian style about your duty, and then never doing it? But perhaps ye think that a Swiss wouldn't make a good husband, and ye don't want to trouble any lady with a bad house-fellow."

"Oh! that can't be the reason," interrupted a middle-aged English lady, who was blessed with two unmarried daughters. "The Swiss make very good husbands. Some of my friends married in Switzerland. Don't your countrymen make good husbands, Mr. M—— ?"

"I believe so," laughed the questioned bachelor, who, by the way, was a flaming patriot.

"And how is it with the French?" asked the doctor. "What sort of a Benedict does a Frenchman make, ma'am?"

"Oh, a very bad one. I never would marry a Frenchman."

"Well, and the Germans?" continued the Irishman. "Come, we must find out the latitudes and longitudes that produce the best husbands."

"Why, the Germans do very well, I believe," said the lady. "Is it not so, Mr. M—— ?"

"No, Madame. I think the Germans bad husbands —certainly very far inferior to the English and Americans."

"Indeed! You surprise me," returned the Englishwoman; "I thought they were such good-natured men, and so sentimental."

"What do they do to their wives, Mr. M—— ?" broke in the doctor. "Come, what is it that these German fellows do to their wives?"

"That is just the difficulty, doctor. They do nothing at all to them, good or bad; they leave them perfectly alone, and pass their time studying, or hunting, or gossiping in the beer-houses."

"Well, that's bad, to be sure. What an outrage on the sex, to neglect it for beer, rabbits, and philosophy!"

To perceive the doctor's last hit, it must be understood that Mr. M—— was himself a philosopher, one of those enthusiastic scholars who honor the great German race by their daring thought and tenacious industry of research. He was elaborating even then a system which, according to his belief, comprehended Nature, and explained the evil which is in the world.

When the doctor left Bex, I ran out to the omnibus to get a sight of his marvelous overcoat. "There it is," said he, holding up the original garment with the pride of a successful inventor. "Now, how many shirts have I got in here?"

"Four."

"Right. And how many shoes?"

"One pair."

"Right.   And how many socks?"

"Six pair."

"Wrong.   Four pair of socks, one pair of shoes, six shirts, and a couple of handkerchiefs.   That's jist enough for convaynience, and not enough for trouble. Don't ye see?   Good-by to ye."

I soon followed him to Paris to meet my expected letters.

CHAPTER XVII.

DINNERS AND DINERS IN PARIS.

I SHALL make short work of Paris. Dick Tinto has been there with his brush, Mr. Jarves with his spectacles, and Sir Francis Head with his wonderful faculty at picking out the odd sticks of French existence.

Strolling down the Boulevard a few days after my arrival, I stumbled over my old comrade Neuville, whom I had left nearly a year previous up to his neck in Silesian fountains. Neuville remained about ten months at Graefenberg, including an entire winter, and only took flight when Priessnitz died, and Madame undertook to carry on the establishment herself. "Good heavens!" said he, "I don't see how I stood it. I cut my hair an inch long, and cut my hat altogether. We had three feet of snow, and frosts sharp enough to make a white bear whine. We used to slide down the Graefenberg hill on sleds; all of us had sleds, and most of us had no hats: you never saw such a set of maniacs."

Anxious for the honor of hydropathy, I asked him how it was that Priessnitz, who had cured so many others, should happen to die himself. He said that the disease was some internal disarrangement, caused by the kick of a horse many years before; that the brave old fellow fell in the breach, as it were, taking his cure and his usual walk up to the very day of his decease. It was no new malady, then, that overcame

H 2

him; it was the one against which he had been com-
bating for a quarter of a century; the one, in fact, which
had led him to invent his peculiar system of treatment.
He had raised himself from a bed of helplessness, but
he could not entirely rebuild his broken constitution,
and at last death was the conqueror.   During a year
or more he had foreseen his imminent dissolution, and
had even warned the citizens of Freiwaldau not to
build too largely; for, said he, I shall soon be gone,
and then you will see no more of these invalids who
now buy your goods and fill your houses.   It fell out
as he had expected; for after his death, after the mighty
funeral which then covered the slope of Graefenberg,
there was a rapid dispersion of those hundreds whom
his fame had gathered.   He left a famous name, a
worthy name, but no successor.

Neuville took flight with the others, and went to Italy, from whence he had recently come on to Paris.
I asked him where he was staying.

"In an English family—a widow lady and her brother; very good-hearted sort of people; queer woman,
though—very queer.   You had better come round."

I went round and saw Mrs. Keene, a tall, thin, an-
gular woman of nearly forty-five, with the remains of
decent looks about her, and a sufficient air of amiability to recommend her as a landlady.   The rooms were
excellent and well furnished; the street, Rue Castig-
lione, was one of the finest in Paris.   After three
quarters of a year passed in French society, I felt just-
ified in exposing myself to the contact of a little English.   I therefore migrated to Mrs. Keene's from my
hotel, to the great discontent of the landlord, who re-

venged himself by refusing to inform my tailor and shoemaker of my whereabouts, thus delaying me a few days in the receipt of boots and pantaloons.

Mrs. Keene was at bottom a thoroughly English character, of London make originally, but greatly modified when I knew her by foreign experiences. She misused the *H* occasionally, and inflicted various other unfilial outrages on her mother tongue. She was particularly aggravating toward the long words, dragging them into the conversation, so to speak, by the hair of their heads. It was curious to observe, also, what a confusion had taken place in her ideas of the ethics of society, in consequence of a sort of blending of French and English moralities. I could really give no idea of the contradiction of her judgments on various Parisian scandals without detailing long tea-table conversations, too dull for repetition. Sometimes a runaway wife would be horribly mangled by her virtuous criticism, and then, again, a similar culprit would be pardoned, as having " served her husband perfectly right, and good enough for him." But she was always and unchangeably savage on young men who had the bad taste to hang around " them nasty *grisettes*." The *grisettes*, be it understood, are the shop-girls and sewing-girls of France, a set very generally disposed to enter into flirtations with wealthy young foreigners.

We soon found that we were not quite so well off in Mrs. Keene's household as the first few days gave us reason to expect. We were not absolutely starved, nor very much stinted, but there was such an evident scarcity of provisions that we were often tempted to dine out. By the time we had finished eating, the board was generally bare, for the unwillingness with which our landlady dealt out the last morsels was one of the most piquant sauces in the world; enough, as a French gastronome would say, to make a man eat his own grandmother.   I believe that she took a dislike to my character, the sum total of which, in her eyes, amounted to an atrocious appetite.   She used to glance at my empty plate with suppressed indignation, and then ask me if I would take another *small* piece, accentuating the "small" in a manner which seemed to say, "For pity's sake, don't take it; you eat me out of house and home."

She was much more frank in attacking the same defect in her brother, observing snappishly, "There! that's all you are going to have; you make me ashamed of you."

He was a queer, comical little man, this brother of hers; a chirrupy sort of gossip, full of laughter and stories, and impertinently indifferent to his sister's "lengthened sage advices" against over-feeding; a good fellow, in short, who would eat the last morsel on a plate with as little compunction as the first.   He had been a tutor in various wealthy families, and now gained an inadequate living by teaching English to Frenchmen and French to Englishmen.   We used to hear a great deal from this talkative couple about the racing-book of a rich brother in England, about the carriage Mrs. Keene had when she was a married lady in India, about certain lofty acquaintances of theirs in Paris who never came to see them; and we actually enjoyed the honor of taking a thin cup of tea with a young lady of conceited manners, who, according to Mrs. Keene's story, was the sister of another young lady, "which" (still following Mrs. K.) had married a French duke of lofty nobility and immense fortune.

At first, Neuville and I used to light our cigars cheerfully after dinner, and laugh ourselves tired over these little convivial absurdities; but constant repetition finally made them irksome, and by the end of a month we left Mrs. Keene's apartments for more generous quarters. We found some fine rooms in the Rue Rochefoucauld, where we could be served with meals at home, or go out to the restaurant, just as our momentary fancy decided. Our landlord and landlady here were two of the most simple, unsophisticated, good creatures that ever talked French. Father Pipelet, as we called the husband, was a round, fat, addle-headed man, as bashful as a sheep, and infinitely more awkward. He was forever buying the wrong things for dinner, knocking plates off the table, spreading the cloth rough side upward, and butting his ribs against the door in trying to back respectfully out of our apartments. If we laughed at him, he got into a thorough fidget, and danced about with a grin little short of idiotic in its helpless embarrassment. Mother Pipelet was the man of the house, and, like Mrs. Bagnet, always knew beforehand her husband's opinion.

Neuville was at that time nearly as ignorant of French as I had been when I reached Divonne; but our hosts soon devised two ingenious methods of making their utterances comprehensible to him. Mother Pipelet founded her system on the hypothesis that he was hard of hearing, and so, putting her mouth close to his ear, she shouted loud enough to make a mummy hear through his wrapper, after which she drew back dubiously, and fixed her great black eyes on him with an expression which seemed to say, " Well, I think I spoke up high enough that time; I think he understood me a little."

Father Pipelet's plan was still more primitive and comical.   He talked baby-talk to my friend—just such jargon as French nurses prattle to French bantlings. Imagine Jonathan Slick discoursing in a caressing tone to some good-sized foreigner, trying to make English easy to him by calling him "Georgy porgy," and asking him, " Does the ittle manny panny wanty eaty in the housy pousy to-day?"   Communications thus expressed usually set us a laughing, whereupon Father Pipelet got helpless with embarrassment, and ended by popping out of the room with the confused hurry of a roasted chestnut jumping out of the ashes.   This nursery style of conversation, by the way, is sometimes used by the Syrians in talking to missionaries who are not yet well posted up in Arabic.

Neuville and I made a tour of inspection among the Parisian eating-houses, from the lowest to the highest, commencing with an extravagant repast at the *Trois Frères.*   We next devoured our way through the middling restaurants of the Palais Royal, paying two francs for a dinner of four courses with *vin ordinaire,* or two and a half francs for the same with a half bottle of Chablis.   But there were too many people in these establishments—too much uproar and too scant service; the beef was tough also, and had a flavor which reminded us more of omnibuses and city pavements than of plows and green pastures.   Notwithstanding

such disagreeable premonitions of the style of gas-
tronomy to be found in the inferior eating-houses, we
resolved to see the bottom, and went on in our explo-
ration until we had satisfied or disgusted our appetites
cheek by jowl with the blousemen.   The cheapest
foraging place that we found was a little shop not far
from the Post-office, where for two sous we got a bowl
of cold rice and milk, seasoned with powdered sugar,
giving an extra sou for a supplementary roll of bread.
This dish was really so good that I continued to favor
the place with occasional visits, until I heard some
horrible stories about the nature of the milk to be
found in such inexpensive localities, in consequence
of which relations, not wishing to load my stomach
with too much chalk and calf's brains, I gave up rice
and milk for a season.

In an obscure back court a little way from the
Palais Royal there was a small eating-house at which
a *table d'hôte* was served for one franc a head, with
five sous additional for a dessert.   The table-cloth
was always rich with great stains of soup and wine;
the furniture was of unpainted wood, and of the coarsest
fabric; the room was lighted by dim windows, or still
dimmer lamp flickers.   The customers were a grade
or two above blousemen, and seemed to be master
mechanics, shopkeepers from both city and country,
clerks, poor lawyers, and small authors.   At five
o'clock a skinny waiting-maid entered from the kitch-
en and delivered the programme of the forthcoming
meal in a nasal, monotonous tone, undisturbed by the
slightest punctuation.   " There is to-day bean-soup
boiled mutton ham and cabbage also a dessert of

cheese and raisins or of orange preserves." As usual
in French dinners, half a bottle of wine was furnished
gratis, but it was sour enough to draw squeals from a
Hindoo saint or a Pawnee brave.

The worst fare that we found was in the Quartier
Latin, at a *table d'hôte* much frequented by students.
In the first place, the barley-soup very nearly turned
us out of doors by its burnt and stale odor.   Then
came a dish which absolutely confounded our zoologi-
cal knowledge.   It was not beef, it was not veal, nor
mutton, nor hare, nor chicken, nor any thing that we
had ever tasted before.   It was too large-boned to be
of feline extraction, and we shuddered as we questioned whether it might not be mastiff or spaniel.   One
mouthful was enough; and, paying our dues, we departed.   I believe that it was this adventure which
disgusted us with culinary investigations.   We finally settled down on the restaurants of a middle class,
something better than the *Mille Colonnes*, and not so
showy as the *Trois Frères*, but in which we could
command for three or four francs a bottle of the best
vin ordinaire and a most excellent dinner.

We took a great affection to the Café Jouffroy, and
during a long time haunted it regularly in pursuit of
our breakfasts and after-dinner coffees.   It faces on
the Boulevard Poissonniere, while its side doors open
into the Passage Jouffroy, one of those fine glass-roof-
ed arcades, like small crystal palaces, which so brill-
iantly vary and adorn the promenade scenery of Paris.
Here it was pleasant to walk in the cool or rainy evenings, watching the shoals of loungers who drifted up
and down the passage, or staring into the elegant lit-

tle shops which lined it. The three saloons and the numerous marble tables of the café were occupied even to crowding at evening by scores of young men, old men, ladies even, or what purported to be such, all playing eagerly at dominoes, chess, and draughts, or chatting vociferously over *café noir*, ices, and punches. One particular corner was generally filled by a knot of old fellows, respectably-dressed men of sixty or seventy—worn-out beaux, I imagined—who played dominoes with indefatigable interest, and occasionally quarreled outrageously over that insignificant amusement. At eleven o'clock their nurses or housekeepers came for them, and hurried them home with a tyrannical punctuality which was extremely amusing. "Alive ridiculous, and dead forgot," I could not help repeating, after Pope, as I contemplated this infantile close to what had been most probably the good-for-nothing life of a bachelor idler.

We sometimes patronized the middling hotels of Paris, taking pains to select those which were not frequented by Americans and Englishmen. At one of these *tables d'hôte*, where we oftenest dined, there was a jovial set of boarders, among whom we easily made acquaintances, and passed a convivial hour pleasantly. At the head of the table usually sat a Greek, an unlucky gentleman, who had come to Paris to obtain the discharge of some relative from the army of Algiers, and who thus far, as I privately heard, had only succeeded in discharging all the money from his pockets. Opposite us sat a round, jolly Austrian baron, who ate fearful quantities of mustard, and laughed himself crimson in the face over sly hints and broad stories hardly

choice enough to be repeated.   On my right was an
old French captain, long since retired from service, an
endless narrator of anecdotes, and as garrulous as a
bobolink.   Farther down were three young Englishmen, robust clerks from London, gravely disputing
whether they could possibly get drunk on *vin ordinaire*, and concluding that humanity was unable to
swallow enough of it to produce that delightful result.
The captain talked fluently and enthusiastically on
elegance of manners, which was a kind of religion in
his estimation, or at least constituted no small part of
respectability.   "Helas!" said he; "it is almost lost
from France; our young men show nothing of it; they
behave like a set of *commis-voyageurs* (traveling clerks).
Manner is a great art, *Monsieur;* almost a nature, in
fact; a man must acquire it so early that you may say
it was born with him.   Let him grow up without it,
he never seizes it, no matter what society he keeps,
and you can detect him for a native boor the moment
he enters a drawing-room.   Yes, *Monsieur*, a man
must be born to society, or he can not be worthy of
it; he must have it in his blood, as it were."

"But Beaumarchais?" I said.

"Beaumarchais! ah! Beaumarchais?   Eh! well,
that creature had infinite wit, but he was no gentleman; after all, *Monsieur*, he was no gentleman."

The captain was so evidently a relic of old times
and old manners in France that he interested me greatly.   He had a polished and elaborate courtesy of address, united to a jovial lightness, almost levity of
thought, altogether like what I had imagined of the
men who bowed and gossiped in the saloons of Paris

before Louis XVI. mounted the scaffold. Traces of great beauty remained in his face, features of feminine delicacy and regularity, a color still florid, and dark hazel eyes, not yet greatly dimmed by more than eighty years of battle, exile, and perhaps poverty. He had been a refugee in England subsequent on the fall of the old monarchy, and, under the Duke of York, had fought for the *ancien régime* against the armies of the Convention.

One of his campaigning reminiscences introduced a subject to which I have heretofore distantly adverted. "I have often eaten horseflesh when nothing else was to be had," said he, "and I must tell you that the common prejudice against it is an injustice."

"How! was it so good?" I asked.

"Eh! well, not particularly good, perhaps; but, then, why was it not good? Not because the meat itself was bad, but because we prepared it badly. Behold me, for instance, on the field of battle, the baggage-carts several miles in the rear, but mangled horses lying all around me. I cut a fine slice from one of them; but how am I to cook it? The best I can do is to stick it on a bayonet and hold it in the fire. It gets smoked, and there is neither salt nor sauce. When it is scorched on the outside, I must eat it, although it is raw within. You can understand, from all this, why soldiers rarely find horseflesh to their taste. But let it be of good quality, and properly cooked, and I promise you it would be excellent eating."

"Precisely, *Monsieur le Capitaine*," said the baron, who had been listening attentively from his side of the table. "Horseflesh is good. We eat a great deal of it in Vienna; not under the pretense of beef, as it is eaten here, but horseflesh in good faith, sold by its proper name. If you should go to Vienna again," he added, turning his spectacles upon me, "you must try some of it. But let me advise you not to touch the soup. The steak is fair; the roast is excellent; but the soup is worth nothing—absolutely nothing," he repeated, with a grimace of grave contempt.

"Possibly they do not prepare it rightly," said I, with a seriousness suitable to the importance of the topic. "I am acquainted with a gentleman named Count de G——, whom I met at a hydropathic institution. He gave me some delightful information on this very subject. Traveling by diligence in the south of France, he met an individual who proved to be the agent of a flourishing establishment where thousands of old horses are annually turned to the most valuable philanthropic purposes. Not a particle of the animal, according to this gentleman, is thrown away as unservicable. The bones are converted into blacking; the blood affords Prussian blue; the skins are useful for various purposes; a portion of the carcass is boiled to grease; the coarser residuum produces manuring substances; the steaks are excellent; and the soup— *oh, mon Dieu!* the soup is delicious. The agent actually smacked his lips and rolled up his eyes at the recollection of that exquisite *potage*."

All this while our landlord stood behind the baron's chair, scratching his round head in a fidgety anxiety to introduce some remark of his own. "Yes, gentlemen, yes," he broke in at the first pause, "there is a great deal of horsemeat eaten, and here in Paris too. Why, I have it from one of the officers of the Octroi that three hundred pounds of it are imported into the city every day.   All this comes in as horseflesh; it pays duty as horseflesh; it is sold as horseflesh; and it *is* horseflesh.   Then, as to the quantity smuggled in and eaten for beef—*oh, mon Dieu!* nobody knows how much that is."

I will just observe that these statements were all made in good faith, and that I consider their truth highly probable, if not certain.   After all, was not the conversation just as absurd, to the true cosmopolite, as would be a discussion between three or four Hindoos as to whether beef could possibly be used as an article of human diet?

The baron was an old bachelor, but so fond of the other sex that it was a marvel how he had escaped marriage.   If a woman of at all passable exterior appeared at our table, he was in a fever to commence a flirtation with her.   He used to joke Neuville and myself on the subject of *les affaires du cœur* with fanatical perseverance, eating, talking, and laughing all together until he was scarlet in the face with mustard and merriment.

Like almost all Germans, he was passionately fond of music.   He seemed to hold great composers and singers in about as much reverence as great poets and orators.   He told me, with some pride, that a country house of his father's once had the honor of covering, for several months, the head of the immortal Beethoven.   "He was quite deaf at the time," said the baron, putting his forefingers to his ears in expressive gesticulation ; "but he still composed, he still thought out his harmonies, although he could not hear the sound of an instrument.   He had the air of a man possessed, for he walked about in a perfect abstraction, waving his hands and muttering bom, bom, bom, bom. I was very young then, but I well remember his looks, for my father used to point to him and say, 'My son, you are a little boy now, but as long as you live you must never forget that you have seen that great man, the immortal Beethoven.' "

CHAPTER XVIII.

FLORENCE AND ITS CASCINE.

FLORENCE! I seldom hear the word without at least a faint semblance of that emotion with which a man hears the name of the mistress of his heart. For me, no other precinct of this earth verdures so greenly in memory, or beams so brightly in the sunlight of imagination, or has made me love it so when I can hardly tell why. There seemed to be an affinity with me in its very air, an interest like that of recollection in all its scenery, as though my spirit had been born there in other centuries, and had possessed there long ago a country, a history, love, joy, sorrow, and death. I have seen otherwheres climates more serene, landscapes more Eden-like, palaces more magnificent, art equally glorious, and women as beautiful, yet never have I met in any other spot all these things blended so evenly, and forming a whole so unmarked by any gross deficiency. If there be any assignable cause for the fascination which Florence exercises over almost every man of susceptible feeling, it is this union, so nearly complete, of a beautiful nature in all its elements with a beautiful art in all its forms. And added to this splendor is a history full of the finest human interest, fragrant with a breath of genius such as perfumes the walls of no other modern city. Who that walks in Florence shall forget the visions of Dante, and the love of Petrarca, and the mirth of

Boccaccio, and the artistic sublimity of Michael Angelo, and the starry glories of Galileo?

The breath of Florence seemed to reach me long before I came within sight of its domes and campaniles. No more grating northern winds, no more half-frozen rains pursued me, but a warm whisper of air, as from southern seas and drooping tropical palms. When we halted at the way-stations of the rail-road which runs from Leghorn up the valley of the Arno, the evening breeze flowed in upon us from gardens overbrimming with the perfume of flowers. The soft tones of the Tuscan, a language of nightingales, fell like fairy music on my hearing, all the more entrancing after so long a period passed without the circle of its melody. In fact, I was drunk with pleasure at finding myself again in Italy, and breathed out joyously one of those favored hours when earth becomes idealized, and all realities put on their halos of poesy, like snowy mountains grown warm and rosy with the rich glory of sunset.

The next morning the gray, practical tints of existence had resumed empire, and I turned my attention to the actualities of Florence. I am not so sentimental, thank Heaven! but that I can generally eat my breakfast, and digest it into the bargain. Neuville, an individual who, like myself, has a body attached to his soul, accompanied me in the spirit of hungry fellowship to the *Café Doney*. It was just the same thing as ever, from the three saloons, the cream-colored columns, and the marble-topped tables, to the white uniforms of Austrian officers, the easy traveling coats of English tourists, and the noisy waiters, rushing about like incarnations of perpetual motion, and shouting the orders of the guests with the vehemence of sea-captains in a hurricane. Giovanni, the good-natured fellow whose particular duty it was to pour out the coffee, came up to us with a grin of friendly recognition on his face, a huge coffee-pot of welcome in one hand, and a hospitable vessel of hot milk in the other.

"Good-morning to these gentlemen," said Giovanni. "They are welcome to Florence. I hope they have had a pleasant journey. What will they take for breakfast?"

We mentioned our wants: "Two coffees, four eggs, and bread and butter!" repeated Giovanni at the top of his voice, as if it were important that all Florence should know what the two gentlemen were about to eat. In response, another waiter soon appeared from a back room, bringing all the appurtenances necessary to the comfortable devouring of two coffees, four eggs, and bread and butter. "Mix!" trumpeted this fellow, now that it was his privilege to roar. "Mix!" echoed Giovanni, with the shout of an avalanche, thereupon pouring in the correct proportions of coffee and milk with the dexterous rapidity of long experience. Then both darted away to offer the same boisterous hospitality to other customers, leaving us face to face with two coffees, four eggs, and bread and butter.

"*Giuseppe!*" shouted Neuville to a long, gaunt waiter, who appeared to be made of bean-poles for limbs, with a weather-cock for a head.

"*Signore!*" exploded Giuseppe, in an astonishing bass voice which would have done honor to a *basso profondo* in a tragic opera.

I

"*Galignani.*"

"*Si, Signore.*"　And away went Giuseppe with the movement of a kangaroo, in search of the famous English journal of Paris, the instructor and consoler of wandering Anglo-Saxons throughout the Continent. Giuseppe's voice was a remarkable affair of itself, but still more so when compared with the small cubic capacity of the carcass in which it dwelt. He made one think of an oboe, or a trombone, or any other lengthy, slender, and sonorous wind instrument. It seemed as if he must be hollow from head to foot to admit of the production of such a quantity of sound. He was long enough for it, in all conscience, but not half wide enough nor thick enough. He was as flat down his breast as down his back, and, in fact, rather flatter; for his bust was like a pancake, while his shoulder-blades were plainly perceptible. He had no seat to his pantaloons, and might have worn that garment hind side before without inconvenience, so that it was wonderful what he found to sit down upon, unless it were the lower extremity of his back bone. His cranium stuck well forward, like the figure-head of a vessel, and, being set on a long neck, seemed to appear around corners or through doorways a considerable season before the arrival of the body, as if, in fact, it were migrating about on its own account, and belonged to nobody in particular. It was trimmed with short, black, bristly hair, variegated slightly by gray; was perforated with a mouth of the largest calibre, very useful, aside from other purposes, for making grimaces to amuse favorite customers; and exhibited, by way of frontispiece, or, more properly speaking, pref-

ace, a lengthy hawk nose, which, not to put too fine
a point on it, was usually rather snuffy. Neuville declared that he bore a striking resemblance to storks,
cranes, and that kind of bipeds, and pretended to be
surprised that Giuseppe did not scream like a heron
or boom like a bittern, instead of enunciating melliflu-
ous Tuscan.

Presently there waved in the doorway of the café a
broad-brimmed Leghorn hat, perched on the head of a
full-formed, robust girl of twenty or twenty-two. A
face agreeable rather for good-humor than for beauty
looked out from under the dancing straw braid, and
smiled on the new-comers. It was Enrichetta, the
youngest and prettiest of the flower-girls of Florence,
bearing on her round, vigorous arm a broad, shallow
basket, brimming with little bouquets of exactly a button-hole circumference. Her pulpy lips parted, dis-
closing a gleam of white teeth, as she advanced with
an easy, confident air to our table. " Good-day to
these gentlemen. How happy I am to see them returned to Florence! Will they take some flowers?"

Here a dexterous movement of her hand translated
a couple of nosegays from her basket to our button-
holes; and then, scarcely pausing to accept of a small
piece of silver, Enrichetta passed on with a smile and
a nod to the next table. I could see that during my
absence of two years from Florence she had greatly
improved, not only in dress, but in her style of carrying herself and presenting her flowers. But there were
several scars on her chin and throat which somewhat
marred even her rustic style of beauty; and I soon
learned that, about a year previous to this our meet-

ing, the current of her life had been rippled by a most
serious adventure.   There was an older *fioraia*, named
Erminia, still good-looking, and once, I was told, beautiful.   She spoke a little tolerable French, some words
of English also, had a graceful address, and was long
the public favorite.   But Erminia found herself verging toward thirty, while Enrichetta was becoming every year a more formidable rival.   Jealous both in
heart and purse, the elder *fioraia* resolved, with the
true ferocity of an infuriated *Italiana*, to deface her antagonist's beauty, and so drive her out of the market.
She made use of her husband as an instrument, and
urged him on to violence in the spirit of a rustic Lu-
crezia Borgia.   The rascal actually assaulted Enrichetta in the café, and cut her throat with a pair of
flower-scissors, as if she were a rose or a marigold, injuring her so severely that she was confined for weeks
to the hospital.   But the triumph of violence was
short, however sweet, for the Tuscan law, with a singular eccentricity, interfered on the right side, for once
falsifying the joke of the Florentines, who, pointing to
the statue of Justice on the lofty column in the *Piazza
della Trinità*, are accustomed to tell you that justice
is out of their reach.   The throat-scissoring rogue
went to prison, while Erminia was ordered never again
to enter or pass by the Café Doney.   This was very
nearly a death-blow to her business prospects, as it is
precisely in and about this café that genteel loungers
in Florence, foreign and native, most do congregate.

. Thus, when Enrichetta was able to resume her occupation, she found herself queen of flowers in the
city.   There was, indeed, another *fioraia*, Giuseppina,

who had in her day been the belle of the profession. But Giuseppina was now full forty-five years old, and, what was even worse, sustained the unpopular reputation of being a government spy, having, in fact, been nearly lynched as such by the victorious Democrats of 1848. Consequently Enrichetta now had a capital time; distributed a profusion of flowers, and got well paid for them; dropped her old awkward timidity, and picked up an easy lorettish forwardness; treated herself to a large variety of dresses, woolen, calico, or even silk, and filled them handsomely; was very intimate with the Florentine dandies, and joked with them in a style altogether too free for translation; and finally, after the fashion of the *fioraie*, accepted the lucrative addresses of various generous-hearted admirers. Two of these Corydons were Greeks, both of whom had the impertinence to quit Florence after a while, in contravention of their vows of eternal fidelity. Enrichetta, in consequence, considered herself an injured woman, and permitted herself the singular freak of hating the whole faithless nation. A phil-Hellene no longer, she never knowingly gave a flower to a Greek; and it was in vain that an Athenian friend of mine once tried to reason her out of the unclassic prejudice. His Attic eloquence was useless, and he got no bouquet, nor scarcely even a sulky, unregardful reply.

I have seen flower-girls in other cities of Europe, in Venice and Paris, for example, but none like those of Florence. Every where else they sell their flowers; here they have the air of giving them away. If you offer them money, they accept it, but they never ask for it, and very rarely wait by you as if expecting it;

no, the *fioraia* of Florence has better manners than
that; she drops a bouquet on your table, or fixes it in
your button-hole; then, with a quick glance in your
eye and a flattering smile, she trips hastily away; but
at your departure, while you are stepping into the rail-
road station or the diligence-office, thinking in the joy
of a good conscience that all your creditors are satisfied, you suddenly see before you the *fioraia*, smiling,
wishing you *buon viaggio*, presenting her final bouquet,
and awaiting the reward of her floral beneficence.   A
trifling present satisfies her, for you could purchase
her whole basket of nosegays for half a dollar.   Enrichetta was abundantly content when I gave her a *fran-
cescone* ($1.04), after having been, for more than two
months, a pensioned voluptuary on her roses and jes-
samines; and I, for my part, willingly paid this small
tax for the sake of sustaining so pretty and sentimental an institution as that of the *fioraie*.   What a loss
would its extinction be to Florence, whose very name,
as some say, comes from the word *fiore*, signifying that
it is the city of flowers!   My button-hole always had
a nosegay as I paced the Lung' Arno, or rode to the
Cascine, making me seem, no doubt, like a most lacka-
daisical trifler to every hard, sensible tourist just arrived from severe, stony New England.

And then, O lounger in Florence, if lady friends of
yours come to the city, what sweetest of welcomes can
you send them by the hands of these florist messen-
gers!   Erminia bears them your card in a handsome
bouquet, and the fragrant compliment only costs a
paltry half dollar.   Indeed, the flower-girls have the
credit of carrying more than cards; they are dexterous

intriguers, men believe, and slip many a forbidden love-letter into white trembling fingers. With beautiful profusion, too, and at a trifling expense, do they garland the balls and wedding-feasts of Florence. Giuseppina had the monopoly of such occasions as these, for her skill shone pre-eminent wherever large and elaborate flower decorations were needed. "Nobody can make bouquets like Giuseppina," she said, proudly, showing me a ponderous wreath of supreme elegance. This veteran *fioraia*, by the way, had won a little fortune in her graceful trade, being possessor of a house and garden, besides having set off a niece with the respectable dowry of six thousand *francesconi*.

But I must not sit all day in the Café Doney, gossiping about the *fioraie*. As Giovanni has let out what I had for breakfast, he shall tell how much it cost me. " *Quanto*, Giovanni ?"

" *Si, Signore.* Coffee, two *crazie ;* butter, two *crazie ;* two rolls of bread, two *crazie ;* two eggs, two *crazie. Un paolo, Signore.*"

A *crazia*, be it known, is worth a cent and a quarter, so that eight *crazie*, or one *paolo*, amount to ten cents. Having thus breakfasted for a dime in the most fashionable resort of Florence, I felt generous, and gave Giovanni half a *paolo*, which was such an unusual gratuity that he looked puzzled and hardly dared take it. In a general way you pay the waiters nothing, except an odd *crazia* or two, given every three or four days, and this only when you take breakfast or something else which implies the soiling of a number of dishes. For a simple cup of coffee or an ice, you plank your *mezzo paolo*, and pocket the two odd *crazie* without the slightest shame.   At Paris you can not consume the most trifling refreshment respectably unless you present the garçon with a couple of *sous.*

Doney's café is the only in Florence where the coffee and butter are almost invariably good.   The breakfasting-place next in quality and fashion is a café-restaurant kept by a Swiss named Wital, known to the soft-spoken Florentines by the milder trisyllable Vitanly.   I more than suspected it of being rather dirty, yet I often took my morning meal there, partly for the sake of an occasional beefsteak and potatoes (not procurable at the rival establishment), partly for the company of Hart, Galt, and two or three other artists who favored its rickety marble-covered tables.   In fact, many American travelers dine there, although they could do much better at the restaurants, particularly at the one known as the Luna.   The place was much frequented also by subaltern officers of the Austrian garrison, who made an outrageous clatter of German consonants over their beer and cigars, contrasting strongly with the flowing cadence of the Italians, or the low and somewhat nasal tones of us Americans.

Erminia and Giuseppina rarely came to Wital's, and Enrichetta almost never; but the establishment was hatefully haunted by a homely old creature, who tried to force herself upon a disgusted public as a flower-girl.   Beggars, also, were too common at Wital's, spoiling your breakfast with the spectacle of their sickening filth and the monotony of their doleful whine, patrolling the rooms at will, or, when driven out, gibbering and mowing through the wide windows.

As people (I mean leisurely people) rise late at Florence, ten o'clock generally came before I had finished my breakfast. From that time to five, my ordinary dinner-hour, it was hard work to get rid of the day unless I wrote or studied. There were the galleries, to be sure, the churches, with their historical monuments, and the delightful promenades around the city; but sometimes I was too lazy or too indifferent to be interested even in these wonders. However, five o'clock always came in one way or another, and then I marched off to dine, sometimes at the Luna with Gould, Tate, and Neuville; sometimes at Wital's, with Hart, Galt, and Jackson. My dinners at the Luna cost me thirty or forty cents at the utmost, including a small flask of Chiante or Montepulciano wine, equivalent to good *vin ordinaire* in France. The meal over, we lounged on the sofas, told stories by the hourful, smoking meanwhile cigars of Swiss or Italian make, costing a cent apiece, and well worth treble the money, as cigars go in America. Gould was a capital mimic, a first-rate narrator, and had as many tales at his tongue's end as the inexhaustible sultana of the Arabian Nights. Ah! reader, those were wonderful dinner-hours, worthy of your envy.

The stories out, we lit fresh cigars and set off jovially for Doney's to settle our digestion with a cup of *caffé nero,* that is, strong coffee, sugared, but milkless. It would generally be about dark by this time; but there were days when we dined earlier, or expedited matters at the Luna, so as to give ourselves opportunity for visiting the Cascine. As Gould was the oldest hand in Florence, and knew most thoroughly its

I 2

prices and its trickeries, he was generally appointed to bargain with a coachman. Three or four Jehus, furnished with tolerable teams and barouches, generally stood in front of Doney's. Now and then one of them would nod to us and jerk his hand back, by way of inquiry whether we wanted to drive out of the city. Hereupon Gould held up three fingers, signifying that he was willing to incur the expense of three pauls for the sake of that gratification, to which the Italian inevitably replied by a shrug and a show of seven or eight digits.

"Too much," was our countryman's criticism.

"Oh no, *Signore*, not too much. A good carriage and horses. Come; there is music to-day at the Cascino."

"Four pauls."

"I can not; really I can not. Say six pauls, *Signore*."

"No, five."

"No, no, impossible;" and here the fellow usually started off with a confident air, as if sure of finding greater liberality elsewhere. At the end of a block, however, he was pretty certain to make a circuit and drive up to the steps again, saying, "Well, *Signore*, give me five pauls and a *buona mano*" (present).

"No, five pauls and no *buona mano*."

"Good, *Signore*; it is too little, but get in. If I drive well, the gentlemen will not grudge me a bottle of wine."

In we got; a ragged, toothless old fellow shut the door in hopes of winning a stray *crazia*; two or three dirty urchins picked up the stumps of our cigars and commenced smoking them; and just as Enrichetta flung a trio of nosegays into the carriage, we rolled away down the long street leading to the *Porta al Prato*. Policemen and sentries at the city gate made no objection to our passing, for they had a faculty of divining a man's destination, and they probably knew us by sight. Wheeling to the left, and skirting a small suburb, we came upon a straight road shaded by trees, and lined on one side by a narrow wood, on the other by long green meadows, one of which formed the race-ground of Florence. Omnibuses, hacks, and stylish family carriages, many of them emblazoned with noble family arms, and decorated behind with militia generals in knee-breeches, rattled before and behind us over the hard, even macadam. A tide of pedestrians, men, women, and children, flowed along the pathways under the shadows of the green branches. To the right lay an Italian Eden, tilled to perfect beauty, rich in mulberries and vines, dotted with farmhouses and villas, rising rapidly into verdurous hills, and closing far away in the rough mountains of the Lunigiana. To the left, parallel with our road, although unseen from it, rolled the Arno. Beyond the Arno, visible here and there through openings in the foliage, reposed low yet varied eminences, which were almost human in their mild loveliness of expression. One green hill there was, especially, softened in its contour by numerous oaks, sympathetic with humanity by its convent and cypressed cemetery, which seemed in its touching grace like a *Mater Amabilis*, though browed with the leafy diadem of earth instead of a golden seraphic halo.

The gray-headed Grand-Duke, accompanied by his wife or his infirm sister, met us in an elegant carriage; an unfortunate, helpless Grand-Duke, never cheered and seldom even courteously saluted by his sullen, contemptuous subjects.   A straight course of nearly a mile brought us to an open square, faced on one side by a ducal country house, and on the other by a promenade abutting on the Arno.   Rapidly making the circuit of the *piazza*, our coachman drew rein at last among the scores of carriages which nearly choked up the broad space in front of the villa.   A ring of music-stands already occupied one portion of the square, and around them clustered the white uniform coats of one of those magnificent Austrian military bands, unquestionably the finest in the world.   Within the circle, glancing watchfully over his sixty or seventy subordinates, stood the broad-chested, martial-browed leader.

A few premonitory beats, and the sublime chorus of instruments rolled grandly into one of the finest passages of Verdi's passionate opera, the Trovatore. Oh, such music as then rose through the trembling leaves of the surrounding trees, and floated away on strong wings of harmony over the ripple of the Arno! The restless ebb and flow of pedestrians ceased, and the crowd gathered like a sea of living, listening silence around that island of melody.   Through all the finest strains of the opera ; through its love, jealousy, rage, tenderness, hope, and despair ; through the longing, dying love-song of the Troubadour ; through the awful miserere which shrouds his life in doom; through the last fragile melody at the close, which regretfully echoes of lost liberty and happiness, the wild instruments wandered with a wonderful power and flexibility of emotion. The story unfolded again before us as we had heard it on the stage from Albertini, Boccarde, and Graziani, swelled through all its tempestuous, changeful feeling, and sunk into silence under the last beat of the leader's hand.

The flow of pedestrians around the grassy circle recommenced, the hum of conversation and laughter burst out with fresh vivacity, carriages started from their posts and made the tour of the square to gain some more favored spot. After a pause of five minutes the band struck up a lively waltz to alternate with the sadness of the opera. Thus, on the pinions of music, an hour or two slipped away, until the dimness of twilight sent the thousands of spectators and listeners back to Florence.

If the music ended early enough, we sometimes took a sunset drive to the extremity of the Cascine, where it is closed by a little brook which empties into the Arno. The whole length of this beautiful promenade must be a mile and a half, shaded every where by the same continuity of elms, and faced by an unbroken succession of meadows. There is a road on the bank of the river, another leading longitudinally through the park, and another along its northern outskirt. Pedestrians are plentifully accommodated with paths and with stone benches. In short, the Cascine of Florence is one of the most delightful public resorts in the world, and with the addition of its bands of music, its crowds of carriages, and its thousands of loungers dressed in their holiday suits, is incomparable, not for vastness or magnificence, but for gentle beauty and quiet gay-ety.

When I was at Florence, the music days of the Cascine came four times a week, the great occasion being Sunday. The Austrian bands alternated with the Tuscan ones, no contemptible rivals. *Cascine*, by the way, simply means *pastures*, and the ducal villa which I have mentioned is simply an elegant dairy.

PICTURES.

BEATRICE.

Her life is warm
  With cherished duty;
Her soul and form
  Contend in beauty.

She heeds no lure
  Of idle pleasure;
Her thoughts are pure,
  Her words a treasure.

She smiles upon
  The poor and saddened;
Their hearts are won,
  Their faces gladdened.

She bends her knee,
  A saintly maiden:
Her grave shall be
  A gate to Aidenn.

THE CRUCIFIXION.

A Pharisee and a Sadducee
  Were reconciled that morning,
And wagged their heads with wicked glee
  At Christ in his bloody scorning.

A soldier from the cohort rushed,
  And struck in pagan fury;

The blood and water mingling gushed:
" Save thyself, O King of Jewry !"

The frightened dead disturbed the noon;
The light of heaven diminished;
The earth and sea, the sun and moon
Heard a voice cry, " It is finished!"

CHAPTER XIX.

CERTAIN FLORENTINE LOUNGERS.

MY life at Florence was a pattern which I would humbly propose to the imitation of all loungers in the Tuscan capital. I shall speak of it at some length, as it was admirably adapted to the climate, suitable to my profession of doing nothing, and most truthfully characteristic of the sauntering population by which I was surrounded. The Arno sliding down its long, rich valley, the sunshine sleeping at monstrous length on the vineyard slopes, were not more regally lazy than I, nor enjoyed a more sybaritic luxury of tranquillity. To this luscious *far niente* I was notably incited by the example of my friend Neuville, who confessed to being one of the most indolent men ever raised in Virginia—a state of which Governor Wise, or some other equally impartial authority, has observed that the only industrious animal which it contains is the tumble-bug.

There were whole weeks during which Neuville and I scarcely ever did any thing more violent than pull on our boots or smoke a hard-drawing cigar. We got up at ten, spent a full hour in dressing, and reached the Café Doney early enough to finish breakfast and read *Galignani* before noon. By the time these labors were over, it was quite too hot to walk except on the shady side of the street, for the sky which now lay

above us was the calm, rainless, cloudless, effulgent
blue of the Florentine late spring and early summer.
But we sometimes went down the Via Tornabuoni,
slowly, very slowly, and, making a turn to the right,
entered the vast, solemn quietude of the Duomo.
Marble floors and lofty vaultings here welcomed us
with such a delightful coolness that we could not but
sit down on the benches, to inhale, as it were, the
delicious shadows, and repose our wearied strength,
staring the while at a troop of lazy, white-robed priests
loitering through some incomprehensible service.

A quarter of an hour in the Cathedral refreshed us
sufficiently to enable us to traverse the Via Calzaiuoli,
pass the Piazza Gran-Duca, and reach Neuville's rooms
in the Via Porta Rossa.   On the way we halted beneath
the graceful arches of the Mercato Nuovo, and bought
strawberries, or some of the gigantic cherries of Pistoria, as big as English walnuts, for our afternoon lunch.
Neuville's lodging consisted of two most comfortable
first-story rooms, with a cool northward front, costing
him only seven dollars a month, furniture and service
included.   I had been less fortunate in my selection,
for, although I had large chambers, they were unpleasantly heated by the sun, and thus we generally passed
our mornings in the Via Porta Rossa.   If it was very
warm, we partially undressed, and reposed on the sofas
in a costume which was certainly picturesque, classic,
and comfortable—smoking meanwhile, talking lazily,
reading a little Italian, and so slipping almost uncon-
sciously through the soft hours of breezy summer day.
The chief drawback to our languid enjoyment of this
Castle of Indolence was a persevering tinker right

across the narrow street, who would not lie down and
take the world easy like ourselves, but profaned the
tranquil June air with a remorseless hammering on his
complaining kettles and saucepans.

At two or three o'clock the fat landlady brought our
fruit, which had been cooling itself in a mighty bowl
of water.   Pistoria beats the world in cherries, and the
strawberries, pears, plums, and grapes of Florence are
excellent.   The Tuscan watermelons are not better
than those of New England, and quite inferior to the
same fruit in our Southern States; as for the musk-
melons and apples, the less said on such dry subjects
the better.   Ever since my return I have been sorry
that I did not eat more grapes while I was in Europe.
The grape of Italy is about the same thing with that
of Syria, equally firm, thin-skinned, and tender, equally
removed from our native American production, with its
tough cuticle and its bullet of seeds within, only fit to
shoot alligators.   I also regret, by the way, that I did
not attempt to see the process of wine-making in France
and Italy.   In Syria, the manufacture of extracts from
the vine is not an agreeable spectacle.   I have before
my eyes at this moment a vision of six unwashed Arabs
standing in an enormous vat of grapes, their loose trowsers tucked up to their hips, and their sinewy legs spat-
tered with the precious juice, while a dozen brown feet
stamped in unison among the crushed piles of oozing
fruit.   My brother, the Hakeem, saw one individual
performing this labor with a running sore on his ankle ;
saw another leap out of the vat, rush across a dirty yard,
and then resume his occupation without so much as
scraping his soles.   There are advantages, to be sure,

in the system : it does not express the acrid juice of the stems into the wine ; it cleanses the operator's feet, and comfortably softens his corns.

It was unfortunate for my grape experience in Europe that, during the four years of my residence there, the vine disease prevailed, seriously injuring the crop almost every where, and in some places destroying it entirely. Thus the raw fruit itself was scarce, its products were high, and some species of wine nearly disappeared from the market. This was a terrible affair to the poor peasantry, for the grape is one of their most profitable harvests, while wine they consider a prime necessity of life. Doctor Zanetti, one of the best physicians in Italy, set himself to searching out a substitute, and actually produced the novelty of rum and water, which was heralded about Florence as a wonderful discovery.

Well, in such talk as this, five o'clock finally came in a very lazy way, as if it didn't care whether it ever got there or not, and then, dressing, we sallied out to dinner. At the Luna we passed a pleasant hour, thanks to the very endurable kitchen of that establishment, as well as to the company of Gould and other good fellows whom we generally met there. Then came the cup of coffee at Doney's ; then the drive to the Cascine in the cool twilight ; then an ice and another cigar at Doney's. After this we walked about the city, or repaired to Wital's to talk with Hart, Read, Tait, Sumner, Millard, and the other *habitués* of that social rendezvous ; or we took seats on the wooden benches, which in summer nights were ranged on both sides of the beautiful Carrara Bridge, and looked at the clear evening skies, the long lines of palaces, and the dark river rippled with lamplight and moonlight ; or, if we wanted some more passionate amusement, we repaired to the Cocomero for a comedy, or to the Pergola for an opera and a ballet. By twelve o'clock we generally considered the day creditably improved, and went home to bed. However warm the sunlight had been, the nights were cool and refreshing ; for always at midnight a quiet air stole down from the Apennines, and breathed over the city its reposeful benediction.

Yes, Florence was the only place where I ever thoroughly enjoyed a life of supreme laziness. For the sake of my good name in industrious Yankeedom, I will add that I was not thus indolent all the while. As at Paris, I made some use of the public libraries, and translated English copiously into the language of the country. At one time, with the aid of Minuti, my Italian teacher, I commenced rendering Hawthorne's House of the Seven Gables into Tuscan, an editor of Florence having agreed to publish the same in the *feuilleton* of his weekly journal. A more difficult style to reproduce in an idiom of Latin origin could hardly be found, I presume, in our Anglo-Saxon. The choice epithets and metaphysical ideas of the Pyncheon family's history stumbled us to such a degree that we could only make out about three pages a day ; and, after finishing three chapters and part of a fourth, the work fell through in consequence of my departure from Florence. In fact, it was a little beyond our capacities, for I was by no means a master in the graces of Italian composition, while Minuti, a good prose writer and something of a poet in his own language, could hardly speak a comprehensible word of English.

At the Café Doney I used to meet, besides my American friends, a number of European acquaintances, young fellows of various nations, Englishmen, Frenchmen, Italians, and even Greeks. The foreigners were commonly artists, or, like myself, travelers and loungers. The natives were some of them artists also; some of them members of the Grand-Duke's "Noble Guard;" others young advocates, or holders of small offices under government.

One of the most characteristic specimens of European youth in the set was a Frenchman, whom I shall call Viardot. He was only eighteen, but quite matured; a slender, well-built, easy, lounging lad, as indolent as possible, a little conceited also, yet decidedly clever. He pretended to be a painter, but he never painted more than once to my knowledge, and the result on that occasion was something too bad for a clock-face. In fact, he was too idle to accomplish any thing, being one of that multitude of young fellows in Europe who seem born to the vagrant good-for-naught existence of butterflies. I used to meet him at all hours of the day in the cafés and promenades, when he would salute me with his good-humored smile, yawn immoderately, and declare, "*Je m'ennuie horriblement ;*" after which he proceeded to talk voluminously, until I was obliged to leave him again to his fearful lassitude.

But there was one occupation in which all his indolence left him, and he was capable of showing extraordinary zeal, perseverance, and activity. This was a

flirtation, or, rather, an intrigue, for in Europe flirtation usually takes a serious and practical character.
In affairs of this sort he exhibited an audacity and dexterity really astonishing in so young a practitioner.
He generally had three or four *amoratas* at once, in
different grades of society, from countésses to milli-
ners, so that his time and affections might not be entirely wasted, but find their reward in one place, if not
in another.

At one time he took a great fancy to a pretty, rosy-
cheeked, hazel-eyed little lady, whom I often saw walking the Cascine with her husband, a respectable mer-
cer.   He followed her about the promenades for a few
days, made love to her with his eyes, and discovered
her residence by tracking her home of a Sunday evening.   He next bribed the rascally old housemaid to
inform him of her mistress's hours, and promise him
admission whenever he should call.   One evening I
met him at the café sucking the head of his cane with
an air of baffled disconsolateness.

"Well," said he, "I have made the assault."

"What assault?"

"Why, upon the lady I told you of the other day
—the wife of the shopkeeper.   I have been to see her
at her house."

"Indeed!   How did she receive the compliment?"

"Oh, badly—very badly.   She was not at all flattered by it.   She sent me away broken-hearted, as
you see."

"You do not mean to say that you actually went
to her house without being introduced?"

"But yes.   But certainly.   Listen, and I will relate you the whole affair. You remember I told you how I had bribed the housemaid to let me in. Eh! well, I am not the man to back out; and I was there this afternoon, for my bad luck. I knew that the husband was in his shop, and that my beauty was at home. I halted and rang. My old ugliness came. 'Is your mistress alone?' I asked. 'Yes.' 'Eh! well, go up stairs,' I said, 'and tell her there is a French gentleman at the door who does not speak a word of Italian, and you can not understand him; ask if he shall be shown up.' I let drop a few more pauls into her hand, and she went off, the old image of sin! Presently she reappeared at the top of the stairs, and beckoned me to mount. I was up in two bounds, and found myself at the door leading into the saloon. For a moment my heart was in my throat, and I felt tempted to go back. 'But come, Viardot,' I said to myself. 'The devil! this will never do. You never will be a ladies' man, at this rate.' I composed myself and entered. The lady was alone. I apologized for my intrusion, and then declared my passion before she could get over her first embarrassment."

"You amaze me. What return did the lady make to your immense devotion?"

"What return! Oh, the usual rigmarole. She said she must not listen to me; she said I must go; she said her husband would be home soon; she said I must never hope to see her again; and, what was worse, she held to it, and would not even let me kiss her hand. Yes, my dear, after twenty minutes' hard pleading, I had to give the matter up, and descend the stairs with the consciousness that I had been jumping after grapes too high for me."

"Of course, you drop the affair now altogether."

"Of course not. Why? A man never should consider himself beaten by a first repulse. I shall get my friend Cruzon to present me in form; I have just discovered that Cruzon knows the family well. I shall then have free access to the house, and shall proceed more deliberately. I shall pretend great penitence and remorse, and after a while I shall renew my attack."

He actually followed out this plan, at least as far as the introduction was concerned. But this pretty lady was immovable in her integrity; all Viardot's simulated sorrow and renewed assaults availed nothing.

Another singular companion was Buonacosta, a clerk in the bank. Entering the café, he would sit down to his ice-cream with a disconsolate air, complaining that he was the most unfortunate, the most tantalized man in the world. "So many millions passing through my hands, and not a single million for me! How is it in your country?" he continued, turning to me. "Could I find a stray million there, by any chance?"

"Perhaps you might, my friend, if you could persuade a rich girl to marry you."

"Oh, exactly. So you have heiresses— female millionaires? Are there many of them? Could I come at one easily?"

"Why, there are not so many as to choke up the streets; still, I think I could insure you a girl with a small fortune."

"Oh, I could not think of a *small* fortune. Nothing less than a million! I have set my heart on that little sum, and I must have it, or I shall be a disappointed man."

" Well, there is still one remedy.   Girls with millions are rare, but you could keep on marrying until you had got small fortunes enough to make up your required million."

" Yes, and tickle my wives to death as fast as I got them, like somebody in the story-book."

" No, no.   That plan is dangerous ; it might put your neck in a noose.   You would have to keep your wives until Heaven was pleased to take them of its own accord."

" But that would be polygamy.   Do your laws permit polygamy ?"

" Precisely.   Turn Mormon, and the path is clear. You have heard of the Mormons ?"

" I saw an article on them the other day in the *Journal des Débats.*"

" Well, make a Mormon of yourself; go to Utah, the Mormon Territory, and you will be allowed to keep your wives, and perhaps your money."

" Oh, trust me for that last affair.   I never would be so thoroughly converted as to pay out a single *crazia* for the faith.   Well, I like that plan prodigiously. It suits all my tastes.   Put the wives at a hundred thousand each.   Ten wives make a million ; fifteen wives make a million and a half ; twenty wives make two millions.   Do you hear that, Dini, Bartoldi ? We will all marry ten, fifteen, twenty, fifty wives apiece, if necessary, and then take our wives and our millions to settle in Utah.   And you, Signor De Forest, would you have the kindness to marry forty or

K

fifty wives, and scrape a few millions together, for the sake of keeping us company ?"

"Of course; but I decidedly object to settling in Utah. On reflection, I remember that the Prophet of the Mormons not only calls on the faithful for large allowances of money, but sometimes levies contributions of the handsomest females in their families."

"Is it possible? What a beast that prophet must be, to get a man's hard-earned wives and millions away from him! ' In that case, we will not go to Utah. We will go and populate some country—some new country. Yes, gentlemen, we will gather our wives about us, and go and populate some island or other."

Such was the style of talk of my gay, burly acquaintance, Buonacosta.

The Bartoldi mentioned above was a dapper little fellow, a clerk in the post-office, who, on a salary of less than one hundred and fifty dollars a year, supported a very respectable degree of style as a dandy and man about town. He may have had some other source of revenue, but I always supposed not. Nor did he show any of that disposition to borrow money and to run in debt at the shops which is so common a failing of Young Italy. I fully believe that his little show in the way of dress, canes, and an occasional carriage was all fairly got out of his one hundred and fifty dollars by dexterous management and a perfect knowledge of the markets.

Indeed, he had no reluctance to let us into the secret of his economy, and show us where to obtain merchandise at the cheapest rates. He patronized the inferior tailors, hatters, and shoemakers; and as he could bully these poor fellows, he got his things made well. He wore a black hat in winter and a white one in summer, as well as the richest dandy in town; but he told us that his white hat had served him already three years, by dint of being refashioned and redressed every spring.   His clothes, never of the finest quality, were always neat and well-brushed, and his linen scrupulously clean.   Indeed, taking the small expense into consideration, I regarded his outward man as little less than miraculous for its unspotted tidiness and unpretending gentility.   The only exponent of ostentation about him was his cane, a slender, flexile wand of some foreign growth, which vastly resembled the rest of him in being quite in the style, without costing much.

I never knew where he lodged, and never heard of his dining; but I presume that he had both bed-room and dinner of as good a quality as could be got for a very little money.   He used to appear regularly before Doney's at four or five in the afternoon, jerking his cane or shaking his fingers at one friend after another in the Italian style of recognition, ready to promenade with you on the Lung' Arno, or to step in and take his usual ice or *caffè nero*.   On festas or Sundays he contrived to muster cash enough to treat himself to a drive on the Cascine, or, what was still better, he got an invitation into the carriage of some more opulent acquaintance.   Indeed, I knew by sight at least half a dozen young men, habitual haunters of Doney's, who never were expected to pay any thing in an adventure, as it was well known that they had nothing to pay.   They seemed to have a prescriptive claim on the purses of their friends to a small weekly amount, earning it by their conversation and drollery, or by various little acts of obligingness.

One of my American acquaintances was warned by his landlady not to trust his shopping speculations to the oversight of these friendly dandies. "I know them well," said the suspicious dame; "they pretend to bargain for you, but they really let the shopkeeper charge you what he pleases; and he charges you more on their account, for he knows that they will come upon him for a share."

Bartoldi spoke French fluently, like most of his set, and even had a supportable accent and grammar in English. When I came away, he was bent upon gaining a literary name, and talked constantly of translating English comedies for the Italian stage. The difficulty was to find an English comedy, our language is so wretchedly deficient in good specimens of that kind of literature. He read Bulwer a great deal, especially his short miscellanies, and occasion-ally got out of his grammatical depth in Byron or Shakspeare, usually calling upon Gould or me to assist him back to daylight.

Some of the fashionables of Florence seldom spoke their own language, always using French, even in converse with their countrymen. I remember a short, stocky, fair-haired count, who never in my hearing uttered a syllable of Italian. Another Florentine, whom I met on the steamer from Marseilles to Leghorn, puzzled my fellow-travelers and me during the first half of our voyage by the mystery which he contrived to throw about his nationality. He was a man of past thirty-five, with a bold, reckless air, yet polished and easy, ranging, in short, through all shades of manner, from that of a gentleman to that of a rowdy. He spoke French only, with singular fluency and purity, but still with a slightly foreign taint. He evidently comprehended Italian well, and seemed to have some knowledge of English; had resided in Paris, and traveled in England, Russia, Italy, and the United States. A Frenchman, an Austrian, and an American formed a conspiracy to make this cosmopolite disclose his land of birth. The two former sounded him in turn by adroit questions and leading observations, after which my countryman came out on him bluntly in English, hoping to surprise him into an answer. All useless. But at Genoa a new passenger, a retired Piedmontese officer I believe, recognized our enigma as an old acquaintance. The cosmopolite treated him with undisguised contempt, abusing his country, laughing at his army, and disrespectfully calling the officer himself a *Wooden Sword.* The Piedmontese sought revenge in telling us his friend's history; how he was of a good family in Florence; how he was a great blackguard; how he married a large dowry; how he treated his wife so shamefully that the Grand-Duke sent him out of the country; and how he now wanted to get back again, and make friends with his government and his outraged spouse.

CHAPTER XX.

ECCENTRICS AND ECCENTRICITIES IN FLORENCE.

SOME of the most remarkable specimens of humanity of which I had knowledge in Florence were Englishmen. John Bull has won, all over the Continent, a reputation for eccentricity which I believe to be pretty well merited by the fact. Peculiarities of character show themselves in a man abroad much more boldly than in a man at home; for the former considers himself bound by no laws, no customs—neither by those he left behind him, nor by those of the land in which he is a wanderer. Thus he dresses, talks, and thinks as he pleases; and whoever does this is apt to be worthy of notice, if not of recollection. Thus John Bull, who at home is more independent in his manners than any other person, is doubly so when he finds himself away from his countrymen, and beyond the reach of the *Times.*

I remember one British haunter of Wital's and Doney's, whom, as I never knew him personally, I feel more at liberty to picture—an Irishman, whose name might have been O'Rourke, but was not; he had once worn the epaulets of major in her majesty's service, but was now disabled and pensioned. About sixty years old, he was quite infirm with wounds and hardship, yet still showed a florid face, handsome in feature, but stern and hard in expression, with the traces of a fierce, reckless temper. He had fought I do not know how many duels, and had been invalided by a shot received in one of those honorable absurdities. He used to wander from café to café, leading a little dog now in place of a company of grenadiers, and stumping over the pavement with a peevish, impatient air, as if wrathfully contrasting his present infirm step with the burly vigor of his youth.

I heard him one day telling a friend of his visit to the North Star, the famous steam yacht of our enterprising countryman, Vanderbilt. "He's a regular Monte Cristo, that man; he's the raal Monte Cristo. There niver was any such fellow as Dumas tells about —that's all gammon; but this is the man. Why, he owns a whole fleet of steam-ships; and this North Star is wonderful, the finest thing you iver laid eyes on. A rigular Monte Cristo," he repeated, rising painfully from his seat, and stumping out of the café.

Major O'Rourke had quarreled with Mrs. O'Rourke to such a degree that they finally concluded to divide the world between them, she keeping Ireland, and he holding undisturbed possession of Italy. In such a state of connubial relations, those angel visits, called letters, were naturally few and far between. At last Mrs. O'Rourke died, and the news came to Italy by the journals. A friend of the major happened to observe the announcement, and resolved to break the affair in person to the bereaved husband. He found him in his parlor, at his morning toast and coffee, unusually ill-humored by reason of some fresh twinges in his legs.

"Good-morning, major," said the Job's comforter. "I am glad to see you looking so well."

"I am looking a confounded lie, then," growled O'Rourke; "I've got an infernal pain in my knees."

"Ah! misfortunes never come single," murmured the visitor, taking a seat. No reply being vouchsafed to this consolatory reflection, he recommenced, "Major, have you seen the papers?"

"No; nothing in 'em. What do I want to see the papers for?"

"But bad news sometimes comes by the papers."

"Let it come, and be hanged."

"I mean personal bad news. You might find something in the Galignani of to-day that would touch you, major."

"Not a bit of it; I defy you. My money's all safe —three per cent's—safe as a jail."

"But you have friends, major."

"Don't care a button for 'em."

"But your wife, sir; suppose that you should hear your wife was——"

"Was what?" shouted the major, starting forward, and dropping his toast and butter in his sudden interest; "what d'ye mean? Is the old woman dead? Ye don't mean to say the old woman has actually dropped off?"

"Yes, major; your wife died three weeks ago."

"Now, really, you don't mean to say so! Why, this is the greatest news I've heard in ten years. 'Pon my honor, I'm glad ye stepped in. Take some breakfast. So the old plague is really gone, eh? Well, well, I'm glad to see ye."

Such was the manner in which Major O'Rourke received the first announcement of his wife's decease. But the next morning his physician met him on the Lung' Arno, wrapped up from head to foot in overcoats and comforters, looking particularly dismal.

"Why, major, what is the matter? Out of sorts to-day?"

"Ah! doctor, ye've heard of the old woman's dropping off, eh? Well, it's worn on me unaccountably. Ye're surprised to see me take it so hard, now, I know ye are. Well, she was an infernal old plague, to be sure, but, after all, she was my wife. We lived together like cats and dogs; but we lived together a good while, and it set me aback more than I expected. I thought I'd jist take a blue pill and wrap up a little, in hopes of carrying it off, ye see."

The major's idea was perfectly original, and perhaps very valuable. If Job had only taken a blue pill and wrapped up a little, who knows but that he would have got along under his plagues much better than he did? A new rest for the troubled! a new consolation to the afflicted!

Punctilious Major O'Rourke leads me to the subject of dueling and duelists at Florence. These affairs were not uncommon, in spite of the amiable and rather effeminate character of the people. They generally resulted, however, from some jar between natives and foreigners, more particularly between the Florentines and the officers of the Austrian garrison. It was remarkable that when individuals of these two races came in armed contact, the Germans were oftener worsted than the Italians; a circumstance which I attributed to the superior quickness of a southern eye, and the greater suppleness of southern muscles. The duels were always fought with broadswords, and were

K 2

therefore seldom fatal, although I was told of one which occurred at Leghorn, between a Tuscan and Austrian officer, in which the latter was killed outright.

Another encounter, less serious in its consequences, took place at Florence between an English artist and a Neapolitan duke. The grandee was egregiously frightened, and on receiving a cut an inch long across the first joint of his right forefinger, fell into the arms of his second, exclaiming, "My God! I am a dead man."

A duel in which a good deal of misplaced pluck was shown on both sides occurred between a young Pisan noble, who may as well be called Santoni as any thing else, and an acquaintance of mine named Sergiusti, a member of the Grand-Duke's *Guardia Nobile*. A party, it seems, came off at Pisa, in which some witty sarcasms were dropped by a lady guest concerning the alleged parsimony of Santoni's mother. Sergiusti, greatly amused, repeated them to his friends, who passed them on until they reached the ears of young Santoni. The indignant youth traced the joke back to its starting-point, and demanded an apology of Sergiusti. The guardsman denied that he was accountable.

"I know very well," replied Santoni, "that you are not the originator of the remarks, but you have repeated them. I can not demand satisfaction of your lady friend, and I therefore demand it of you."

"Very good," said Sergiusti; "but give me half an hour. I have just got here. You have danced, and I have not; you have had supper, and I have not. Give me a waltz and something to eat, then I am your man."

The Pisan could not refuse so moderate a request. The guardsman danced and ate while his antagonist looked on. They then repaired to a quiet place, and changed their dessert-knives for broadswords. Sergiusti, a boy of nineteen, was no swordsman, and received almost immediately a cut on his neck, which came as near as possible to chopping his head off. The force of the blow was partly arrested by his parry, partly by his jaw-bone, but it left him with a huge, indelible scar. In addition, the Grand-Duke accorded him three months' imprisonment in the old castle back of his own palace garden, while Santoni only escaped a like reward of merit by hastily leaving the country. Native duelists in Tuscany are generally punished by imprisonment, and foreigners by expulsion. So much for that conventional eccentricity, the duel, as it is managed at Florence.

One of the most original and amusing characters who frequented Doney's was a dog answering to the title of Burrasco. A long-bodied, short-legged dog he was, with a rough black coat, neatly and regularly turned up on the belly, breast, and throat with facings of yellowish white. Of no distinguished breed, I imagine, or rather of no breed at all, he had more sense and drollery about him than any aristocratic dog that ever barked out of a coach window or from the cushion of an embroidered sofa. He had the cunningest stand-up ears in the world, with a perfectly irresistible way of cocking his head on one side, and looking as if he were asking you whether you had such a thing about you as a beefsteak or a chicken-wing. He had commenced life disadvantageously as a coachman's dog, but had totally discarded his plebeian patron, and taken to the life of a Florentine gentleman, frequenting the fashionable promenades, and the most stylish cafés and restaurants. In fact, he was one of those gifted individuals who push their way up in the world from the lowest classes to the highest by dint of personal beauty, attractive manners, and native wit. He was not the only haunter of Doney's who had done this, for I remember a handsome man of twenty-eight, whose brother was still waiter in an eating-house at Leghorn, but who was himself a Florentine buck, and husband of a genteel, well-dowried Florentine lady.

Like many other Continental fashionables, Burrasco slept where he could, which in his case was generally on the pavement. But in the morning he always made his appearance at Doney's full of spirits, and glad to see any body who would oblige him with a slice of bread and butter. Breakfast over, he sat on the steps of the café, played with the other dogs, and barked contemptuously at the ragged boys and beggars. It is no compliment to get a gratuitous bark from a dog; it is pretty good proof that you are ill-dressed, or have something mean or suspicious in your manners. One seldom meets a dog in good circumstances who can bear poor people; he usually barks at them, and, if he dares, bites them. Burrasco at one time got into such a way of assaulting the tatterdemalion urchins of Florence, that he had to be repeatedly chastised for his violence by long Giuseppe and others, who considered themselves responsible for his behavior.

Toward noon this genteel Italian loafer took a nap in the shade, or posted off to a *buffet* called the Terrazzino, to stay his stomach with a luncheon procured from some obliging diner or patronizing waiter. He was so well known and such a general favorite that his mute requests were always attended to, and I doubt whether he passed a hungry hour from morning to night. About four o'clock he made his appearance at the Luna, galloped up stairs on three legs, and walked into the eating-room with a hail-fellow wag of his neat and well-curled bushy tail. If any of his intimates were at dinner, and there happened to be a vacant seat at their table, he forthwith established himself in it, and looked around on the company with a self-possessed yet expectant air, as if he had been regularly invited, and was only waiting his turn to be helped. He finally got so fastidious with good eating that he despised bread altogether, and would touch nothing which was not meat, or at least soaked in meat gravy, no matter what fast had been appointed.

The dinner completed, Burrasco went as regularly as any of us to Doney's. In addition, he learned the music-days, on which occasions, and on no others, he treated himself to a promenade on the Cascine. I doubt whether he cared a shake of his ears for Norma or Louisa Miller, but he listened attentively, with open mouth, sitting on his haunches, amusing himself in the intervals between the pieces by playing with fellow-dogs, or greeting his biped friends with festive bow-wows and capers. When the music ceased, he went back to Florence, like every body else, and generally spent the evening at Doney's or the Terrazzino. In short, from morning to night, year in and year out, his life was so perfectly symbolical of the existence of one of those needy, sponging dandies abundant in Florence, that it was impossible to see the two together, standing side by side, for instance, on the steps of Doney's, without being tempted to laughter by the ludicrous resemblance. Equally lazy and penniless, equally good-hearted, frisky, and toadyish, equally contented with themselves and worthless to the world, the man and dog floated, not swam, down the sunshiny, shallow, sluggish current of fashionable Italian life. Joy to thee, Burrasco! thou wert the worthier character of the two in all clear-sighted eyes, human or heavenly.

There was one species of hospitality, that is, nightly lodging, which Burrasco found it difficult to obtain. He worked hard for invitations, waiting late at the café, and then escorting some particular friend home with a chorus of barks and a multiplicity of capers. Arrived at the door, he sat down and cocked his head on one side, as if turning a favorable ear to the desired offer of admittance. There he remained until he heard the bolt grate in its socket, when he shot off like an arrow to reach the café before it should be deserted, and repeat the same blandishments upon some other human intimate.

He had an amusing way of paying his friends what he evidently considered a polite and grateful bit of attention. Meeting me, for instance, in the street, he recognized me with an emphatic wriggle, and then set off before me, barking furiously, as if to say, "Here's an American friend of mine; get out of the way, you Florentines; give him plenty of elbow-room, or I'll bite you." This complimentary demonstration over, he would give me an inquiring look, to see if I were quite satisfied, and then canter off about his doggish business.

Burrasco was such a general favorite that even the policemen loved him, and neglected to poison him, although by the terms of the grand-ducal hydrophobic law he deserved death, as being a vagrom dog and unmuzzled. Long may this true Florentine gentleman escape official arsenic and private bludgeons, to enliven Doney's and the Luna with his jocose bark and the kindly wag of his curly tail.

A curious book might be made out of the blunders of travelers on the Continent and the impositions under which they suffer. A fine young fellow whom I met in Florence, a Virginian, told me of a rascally yet laughter-provoking trick which was put upon him by one of those guileful coachmen who haunt the paving-stones in front of Doney's. Having breakfasted in the café with a fellow-traveler, he wanted to visit his bankers, Messrs. Maquay and Pakenham. The two called a coachman, and asked him if he knew of the whereabouts of the said firm. The cunning rogue professed ignorance, and sent a boy to the Hotel du Nord, near by, under pretense of inquiring if there were any such people in the city. The boy came back with the direction, as he said, and Jehu, after some haggling, agreed to carry them for five pauls, or fifty cents. They got in, paid the inevitable beggar for shutting the door, and leaned back luxuriously in anticipation of an agreeable drive. Coachy turned his horses, drove across the street, and pulled up. There was

the door, and there was the sign, MAQUAY AND PAKEN-
HAM, BANKERS.   They were indignant, of course, with
the scamp, called him all the bad names they knew
in the language, and refused to settle.   He quietly admitted that the distance was not great, and said, with
becoming moderation, that, " as they were foreigners,
he would let them off for three pauls."   The joke was
worth that, and they handed him the money.

The same friend told me one of his early experiences in the French language and in a French café.
Having, in the course of human events, swallowed one
cup of coffee at breakfast, he called for a second.
"*Tout de suite?*" (immediately?) asked the waiter.
"*Too sweet?*" said my friend ; " not a bit of it.   Bring
me some more sugar."

I made a blunder of a different character during my
first visit to Florence.   Neuville and I, anxious to
learn Italian as fast as possible, resolved to cut all our
Anglo - Saxon acquaintance, and bury ourselves in
some society where we should hear nothing but pure
Tuscan.   We concluded that our best place for attain-
ing this object was to enter a convent—not, indeed, as
monks, but as boarders.   We made pilgrimages to all
the monastic establishments within ten miles of Florence, the Franciscans, the Dominicans, the Capuchins,
and all the other chins or shins that we could hear of.
We rang at the gates, examined the quarters to see if
they suited our tastes, and then preferred our petition
for board, lodging, and instruction.   The holy fathers
usually stared as if they thought us demented, but invariably treated us with the utmost politeness.   " But,
bless you, my children," they always replied, in sub-

stance, "the thing is impossible. The rules of our order do not permit such a step. Besides, how could you live on our poor fare? No wine, no meat; nothing but bread and vegetables. Oh! it would never do for gentlemen like you."

And so they folded their hands over their fat bellies, and blessed us, and sent us away. Our last attempt was on a rusty, straggling conventual edifice, situated on a hill some two miles south of the city. We marched boldly through an open front gate, and were advancing toward the principal door of the building, when the old porter, catching sight of us, ran hastily out of his lodge, crying in an excited way, "What do these gentlemen want here?"

"We want two chambers," said I, briefly.

"Two chambers!" echoed the old man, flinging up his arms in a helpless state of astonishment.

"Yes, two chambers. We wish to practice Italian, and we want company for that purpose. We would like to live here, and will pay well for our lodgings."

The porter was speechless by this time, but his wife came up, and we referred our modest desire to her. The old woman glared upon us a moment, and then burst into a cackle of laughter. "Two chambers!" said she. "Oh! Holy Mother! Oh, God bless me! Two chambers! Body of Bacchus! who ever heard the like? No, no, gentlemen," she continued, shaking the fore-finger of her right hand at us, after the fashion of the Italians when they are very positively negative, "no, no, there are no chambers here for you,

young fellows.   Why, this is a nunnery, gentlemen—
a nunnery!   Ha! ha! ha!"

We backed out of the court in a hurry at this announcement, for fear some devout watch-dog should
be set upon us to avenge our sacrilegious intrusion.
The adventure, no doubt, got among the sisterhood,
and probably excited a good deal of horror and merriment.

CHAPTER XXI.

MARIA AND HER STORIES.

AT the same house where I lived in Florence, on the same floor, in a room farther down the passage, lodged a girl of eighteen or nineteen, slender, generally pale, but with flashing black eyes, and features that were, on the whole, rather pretty. She called herself Maria, was a native of Sienna, and followed the trade of seamstress. As I saw her nearly every day for over three months, we had plenty of opportunities for the exchange of ideas, and I found her an invaluable mine of Italian idioms and Italian credences; for be it known that Sienna is the place, of all Italy, where the language is the purest; and not only this, but it is a retired little city, somewhat away from the great lines of travel and thought, so that old opinions and superstitions still possess there a perceptible degree of vitality. I collected a small museum of ghost frights and witch adventures from Maria's conversation, although such was her timidity and fear of ridicule that she would only relate these wonders by dint of being delicately coaxed and managed.

She was the most bashful girl that I ever saw—bashful with a kind of nervousness, bashful even to disease—and, to the last, she never looked me full in the eyes for more than a lightning-like glance. It was with her face bent down, so as to be half hidden by its own shadow, or by one hand lifted partially over it, that she used to prattle Florentine gossip, or relate her astonishing histories. If I looked incredulous, above all if I laughed, she would stop and declare, with a comical pettishness, that she never would tell me another word.

"Witches? Oh yes, to be sure there were witches. Why, her mother had told her how——" and here, catching a smile upon my face, she came to an indignant stop. "There! now you are laughing at me. I knew you would laugh; I knew you would not believe it. I will not tell you any thing more; you shall not laugh at me."

"No, no, Maria, I am not laughing now; tell me all about it, perhaps I shall believe it. Just tell me the story, and let me see what I think of it."

Then came a most ridiculous narrative, how her mother, when a girl, was very handsome, and thus attracted the evil eye of an old woman of Sienna, who had the name of being a witch. This old woman offered her mother an apple, and pressed it upon her so urgently that, against her better judgment, she accepted and ate it. Consequently, her mother fell sick, and pined away in such a manner as very much astonished her relatives, until they learned the adventure of the apple, when they immediately understood the cause of her illness. Then her father and brothers went to the old woman's house, and, surrounding her with their knives drawn, said, "Thou hast bewitched our daughter and sister, and deservest to die; but cure her, and thou shalt live, and we will promise secrecy concerning thy crime."

So the old woman, in a great fright, went to the chamber of the invalid, and anointed her with some species of ointment which she caused to be prepared for the occasion; after which she kneaded her from head to foot, as you would knead bread, and so brought her out to the family, as smooth, and sound, and handsome as ever. The father and brothers kept their agreement of silence until the witch died, when they felt at liberty to repeat the tale, which had ever since been a current thing at Sienna.

There was a better story of a poor woman who fell partially into the power of Satan through an evil wish. The night following this crime of thought, she was awaked by a tap on the window, and, looking through the glass, she saw a goat which motioned her with one of its fore hoofs to come out. She was under the influence of some terrible charm, for she neither dared wake her husband nor keep her place; and so, rising, she slipped noiselessly through the door, and stood before the strangely potent animal. "Wilt thou harm Christ's earth or his followers?" said the goat.

"I will harm the earth," said the woman, who already repented of her sin, and had no desire to injure her fellow-creatures.

"Then mount on my back," replied the goat. The woman was so constrained by some mysterious power to obey that she instantly bestrode the animal, unable to take any other precaution than that of grasping its long hair. Immediately the goat went off with the swiftness of wind, springing along the bending surface of the cornfields, leaping from festoon to festoon in the vineyards, and galloping madly over the top of the trees. Wherever his feet struck, they ruined every thing, crushing the grain to earth, tearing the vines in pieces, splintering to the roots the strongest olives and mulberries. The miserable rider was bruised and wounded by the crashing branches, her thin robe torn from her in shreds, and her strength exhausted by fatigue and terror, until, after an hour of this fearful aerial gallop, she was brought back to her own door and flung violently from the infernal animal's back. There she lay breathless, unable to move, and with a fearful enchantment upon her of which even she was unaware.

Morning came, and the husband, not beholding his spouse, first called her, then hunted the house over, and finally sought her out of doors. He saw a huge unsightly toad on the threshold, and indignantly kicked it into the bushes. No wife being any where discoverable, he hurried to the neighbors, and told them of this incomprehensible disappearance of his rib. Of course, the poor man's hearth was soon inundated by an assemblage of curious gossips, among whom was the pious old priest of the village. As the holy father trotted about the house, peeping into the most improbable localities for finding a woman, he happened to spy, nestled among the bedclothes, a toad of extraordinary magnitude—so prodigious, in fact, and so abominably ugly, that, in his amazement at the sight of it, the good man incontinently said a *benedicite*. The moment the sacred words were pronounced, the toad changed shape and became the mistress of the house, who immediately proceeded, with many tears and faintings, to tell her lamentable story. She was still dreadfully scratched and pounded from her midnight ride, and had a large bruise on her cheek, caused by the heavy toe of her husband's shoe, so that they were constrained to believe her. The wise father immediately took all the necessary precautions against a second visit from the devil, blessing the house, sprinkling holy water copiously about the grounds, and holding especial service in the parish church that afternoon. These vigorous measures were, by the favor of the Madonna, perfectly successful, and the fiendish goat never troubled the family thereafter with his nocturnal visits.

Another of Maria's stories struck me as really pleasing, and as affording a subject for a pretty night-picture. She said that a pious poor man of Sienna went into the church of San Francisco to say his evening prayers, and, being very tired, sat down on a bench against the wall, where he presently fell asleep. The vespers ended; the worshipers passed out; the sexton closed the dim church; yet the sleeper remained at his post. He was awakened at midnight by a glare of light falling across his eyelids. Greatly astonished to find himself napping in so holy a place at such an hour, he was still more amazed at seeing the altar-candles alight with a halo like that around the head of Christ in pictures, while before them a priest in white robes was in the act of commencing a mass. But, being a man of pious disposition, and, also, not a little awed by the circumstances in which he found himself, he very reverently joined in the service, making the usual responses, and bowing his knees at the proper time. The priest recited with extraordinary fervor, and our Siennese felt unusually edified and uplifted by the holy words, more so than had ever been the case with him on any previous religious occasion. The mass being ended, the priest noiselessly glided to the sacristy, and entered it, without drawing the curtain, or even shaking it by his passage. The spectator hesitated some time between respect and curiosity, but finally stole to the doorway, and, cautiously pushing aside the drooping linen, peeped into the sacerdotal precinct.

At that moment the priest rose from his knees, with a countenance full of unearthly joy, and turned toward him. The Siennese would have drawn back; but when the other, in a low, sweet tone, bade him enter, he obeyed, and stood trembling by the door.

"My son," said the priest, "thou art anxious to know why I celebrate this service alone and at this unusual hour. Know, then, that I am a spirit just liberated from Purgatory, and by thy means. When I died I had one grievous sin on my soul, and that was that I had neglected mass for the repose of one dead; neglected it, too, that I might pass the time in worldly mirth. So Christ condemned me to remain in suffering until I could repeat it in this place, with some faithful Christian to render from his heart the just responses. But until this time no one came, and thus I labored in vain for many years. But now, thanks to thee, and thanks, above all, to our merciful Lord, I have done my work, and am free to ascend to Paradise. The blessing of a purified soul and the blessing of God be with thee! Amen."

So saying, he vanished, leaving his listener wonder-struck, trembling, but, as became a man of his piety, exceedingly joyful at the good which he had been the means of accomplishing. He retired to his bench, and, falling calmly asleep, remained in a gentle slumber until the sacristan discovered him in the morning.

"Did you get this out of a book, Maria?" I asked, when the girl had finished her tale.

"No, no, not out of a book. All the children tell it at Sienna. Every body knows it at Sienna. And it is true, perfectly true. Oh yes."

Another story of Maria's had been related to her, she said, by a very learned lady of Sienna, from which circumstance I have some fears that it may have already appeared in Italian print. It referred to a night-adventure of a young Siennese musician named Martino, son of sober and devout parents, but a youth of very undutiful, vicious, and irreligious character. Being a great spendthrift, this same scampish Martino not only got rid of all the money that he could earn himself, but of all that he was able to beg from his over-indulgent parents. Late one night he came home from a wine-shop where he had been carousing with ungodly companions, and demanded a score of florins, or some such enormous sum, of his mother. The good woman showed him her empty purse, and remonstrated with him on his evil and prodigal ways; upon which the graceless youth got into a rage, and, catching up his violin, ran out of the house, swearing that he must have money, and that to get it he would play the devil's own tune.

It was late now; the wine-shops were shut, the streets were empty, and Martino found himself alone

L

in a city of slumberers.   He walked on moodily until
he came to the Piazza of the Duomo, where he halted
in the shadow thrown on the moonlit pavement by the
marble walls of the fine old Palazzo Saracini.   All the
other buildings of the square were dim and silent, as
usual at that hour; but the windows of the palace
were bright, as if with some ball or other revelry of
extraordinary splendor.   As he stood before the great
portal, a cavalier—a tall, dark man, whom Martino
had never seen before—emerged from the archway
and advanced toward him.   He, of course, wore a
cloak and a slouched hat.   Who ever heard of a
mysterious cavalier at that hour of the night who did
not wear a cloak and a slouched hat?   But he had a
noble port, and a degree of magnificence in his costume
which very much imposed upon Martino's spirit as he
came up and faced him.

"Are you going to a revelry at this hour?" said the
stranger, pointing significantly to Martino's violin.

"I hope so, in the name of all the saints!" replied
the Siennese; "but I very much doubt it.   I am a
poor man, signor," he added, after another glance at
the cavalier's costly cloak.   "I would be glad to earn
a little money; perhaps your excellency could put me
in the way of it."

"Perhaps I could," said the stranger, laughing
with a tone which Martino thought rather disagreeable.   "Well, come with me.   Do exactly as I bid
you, and I will give you more money than you ever
saw.   What do you say?"

"Agreed!" responded Martino, slapping his violin
as if he were to take oath upon it.   The cavalier gave

a sudden stamp on the pavement; the earth and the midnight air seemed to vibrate with a violent shock, and before Martino could cross himself he found that he was inside of what seemed to be a splendid palace. He was astonished at his rapid change of locality, but not unreasonably terrified, for a confused notion came across him that by some legerdemain he had been jerked into a hall of the Palazzo Saracini. The cavalier having disappeared, he amused himself by staring about to see what kind of place the interior of that famous old family mansion might be. It was magnificent enough, certainly; for there were bronze columns, curtains of cloth of gold, and all kinds of splendid furniture and ornaments. But it was oppressively warm; so close, indeed, that he found it difficult to breathe, and the floor was heated to that degree that he could feel it unpleasantly through the soles of his shoes. What puzzled him most was to see this brilliant receiving-hall deformed by long rows of curtained bedsteads, from each of which came, now and then, low groans, exactly as if the place were a hospital crowded with suffering invalids.

"This is odd," muttered Martino; "who ever knew that there were so many sick people inside of the Palazzo Saracini? But, doubtless, I have been brought here to divert them with a little music. I wish it was cooler, though. Who the devil can play a violin in this heat?"

Presently he walked on tiptoe to one of the bedsteads, and took the liberty of drawing the curtains a little to enable him to look within. He was not surprised to discover a man stretched there, but he was very much astonished, indeed, to recognize in him an old acquaintance, a certain graceless elf named Carlo Dinaccio, who had been drowned in the Arno two years before.

"Why, Carlo—friend Carlo," said he, as soon as he could get breath to speak, "what does this mean? We thought you were dead. How came you in the Palazzo Saracini?"

"Ah! Martino," replied the other, in a lamentable tone, "are you, too, here? Have you, too, left the land of the living and come to these abodes of torture?"

"Left the land of the living!" responded Martino. "Not a bit of it. I am as much alive as possible, and so, it appears, are you."

"This is a great mystery," muttered Carlo, with a groan.

"Ay, ay," said Martino, "you are surprised at my having found you out."

"Martino," resumed the other, "do you know where you are?"

"Exactly, old fellow! I am in the palace of the Saracini in Sienna."

"No, Martino, you are in the palace of Satanasso in hell."

Martino made a great jump into the middle of the room, and came very near knocking out his brains or breaking his fiddle in a sudden fit of desperation. Resuming courage as he looked around on the splendid hall, he came back to the bedside.

"But, my dear Carlo, supposing things are as you say, hell is not so bad a place, after all. You seem to be very comfortable here. It is a little warm, to be sure, but quite endurable, notwithstanding."

"Put your hand into my bed," replied Carlo, "and see if I am so very comfortable."

Martino did as he was directed, and twitched out his fingers considerably scorched. "In the name of God, my dear friend, my dear Carlo, who was that cavalier that brought me here?" he screamed; "and how am I to get out of this place? Oh! dear me, how hot it is! Oh! I did not know it was half so hot. Oh! for the sake of our old friendship, Carlo, tell me how I am to get out of this place."

Carlo, for a wicked man and a lost spirit, was wonderfully obliging, and gave his friend the best advice, probably, that he was able. "Be quiet," said he; "you can not escape by force. If you have promised to play at the devil's ball, as I suppose you have, you must fulfill your agreement; but when he offers to pay you, refuse; at all events, only accept so much as he himself puts in your hand. He who stoops to pick up the devil's gold inevitably drops his own soul."

Scarcely had these excellent admonitions been uttered when Martino heard himself called by a voice which he recognized as that of the false cavalier. Casting a parting glance of terror and pity on his lost friend, he sprang to the door, and met his spiritual guide and discomforter. The devil led him silently through a suite of long halls, magnificently adorned, but all pervaded by the same stifling atmosphere. They entered a vast saloon, crowded with people, and mounted a platform, on which the cavalier took a seat, motioning his companion to another. The guests were of both sexes, elegantly dressed, as if of the highest rank, but the most mournful, melancholy set of revelers that Martino had ever imagined. At a signal from the cavalier they ranged themselves in parties for dancing, and at another signal the miserable musician struck up a joyous tune on his violin. The ball opened, and the woeful-looking guests whirled away with a mad rapidity of step which contrasted strangely with the utterly disconsolate expression of their faces.

"Faster!" roared the devil. Faster went the fiddle-bow over the strings, and the dancers' feet over the floor. "Faster! faster!" shouted this energetic master of ceremonies, and each tremendous command extracted new rapidity out of the violinist's elbows and the doleful revelers' knees. Martino's body ached to the end of his nails, but he played on with the perseverance of desperation, until the dancers, one after another, fell exhausted and seemingly senseless on the floor.

When the last one was down, and it was evident that there was not a kick left in the company, the devil patted Martino on the shoulder, and bade him follow and get his pay. He then led the way into another room, one half of which was piled from floor to ceiling with shining gold pieces. "Take what you want—fill your pockets," said he, with a wicked smile. Martino was prodigiously tempted, and resolved inwardly to accept at least all that the devil would hand him. "May it please your excellency to pay me yourself," said he.

"Do not be afraid," repeated the infernal cavalier; "no squeamishness. Take all you can carry."

Martino again objected, and a long contest of invitations and refusals ensued between them. At last the devil, out of all patience, snatched up a handful of the gold and thrust it into the musician's hand. "A thousand thanks," said Martino; "infinitely obliged; and now, if your excellency would only have the kindness to send me home."

"Go!" shouted the devil, and gave a tremendous stamp on the pavement, which made the gold roll down like a yellow avalanche.

In the same instant Martino found himself lying in the street at the door of the Palazzo Saracini. It was almost morning, and the working-people were beginning to glide about the city to their avocations. Martino had a distinct recollection of what had passed, and his arms still ached with his extraordinary artistic exertions in the infernal ball-room; yet he could not persuade himself but that he had been dreaming, until he put his hand in his pocket, and found there thirty or forty pieces of gold, still warm from the fiendish sub-treasury. Then, in a delirium of terror and joy, he rushed home and told his story. It is said that he immediately broke up his spendthrift habits, put his money into business with great success, became a famous usurer, got extremely rich, and finally went to perdition in the ordinary way.

But I should fill two or three chapters if I told all the stories and superstitious beliefs with which Maria amused me. I must observe that she did not relate the above tale in the jesting style which I have given it, but quite gravely, as if it were a very serious history which might be true, notwithstanding certain im-

probabilities.   In fact, she believed firmly in the horns
and tail, and had what might be called a very saving
faith in the devil.

One fancy of hers deserves notice, as it was nothing
less than a desire to have a Bible.   She never had
read the book, and was curious to see what it contained.   I undertook to gratify this wish, and visited
every book-store in Florence, in a vain search after
that anti-papal publication.   There was one edition
of it to be had, indeed, but it consisted of six large
volumes, both too bulky and too expensive for any but
the rich.   Every day, when Maria met me, she inquired
if I had found her Bible.   My barber at last relieved
me from further search by telling me that he could get
me a copy of a small size ; and, coming a day or two
after to my room, he opened his cloak and showed me
a pocket Italian Bible, printed at Malta by the English Bible Society.   He refused to tell me where he
had obtained it, and never ceased to implore me not to
mention the affair to a living soul.   It would be a
great annoyance to him if it were known, he said, and
might ruin the friend from whom he had obtained the
book.

I gave it to Maria, supposing that she would soon
be tired of it ; but, on the contrary, she read it like
a story-book, night and morning, at every leisure moment.   She had some novel on hand at the time, but
the human romance seemed to lose all value by the
side of the divine history, and was thrown aside only
half perused.   The historical parts interested her extremely, as might have been expected ; but she also
read the prophecies and the epistles of Paul with a

vague understanding and a timorous anxiety to catch their full import.   She had no doubts of any doctrine or assertion ; no suspicion as to the full and awful inspiration of the book.   The passages on eternal condemnation, and more especially those on the power and malice of the devil, frightened her horribly, and she almost cried with fear as she read them to me, seemingly with a vague hope that I could contradict them and save her from their terrors.   At the same time, there was a childishness in her interest, and a novelty in some of her comments, which occasionally made me smile.   " Povero Gesú !" (poor Jesus !) she said, when she had finished the story of the Crucifixion.

I left the Bible in Maria's hands with a promise from her that she never would give it up to a priest. I should like to know the future history of that Bible, for there are not so many in Tuscany but that the adventures of one of them might be of some particular interest.   Maria carried it away with her when she left Florence, and it is probable that I never shall hear of either again.

PICTURE.

THE SACRAMENT OF COLUMBUS AT PALOS.*

He kneels upon the chancel pave,
  Madonna's image o'er him bendeth,
The altar candles burn and wave,
  The incense into gloom ascendeth ;
Amid the hushing litanies
  A priest the awful Host extendeth,
And thronging men lift suppliant eyes
  To Him whose word the heavens rendeth.

* Suggested by a painting of my friend, Edwin White.

Along the colonnaded aisles
　　Majestic symphonies are reeling ;
From unknown lands, from nameless isles,
　　They seem, like revelations, pealing ;
A vision floats before his soul,
　　Barbaric hosts and pomps revealing,
Then back the lofty vaultings roll,
　　And heaven shines where he is kneeling.

"O blissful vision ! mortal bless'd !"
　　He sobs through tears unconscious streaming
" The glorious cross ! the cross of Christ !
　　I see it over oceans beaming ;
And God hath chosen me to bear
　　Its light through night, a world redeeming ;
I go, I fly, on wings of air,
　　My life no longer mine esteeming."

He goes, the man of Deity,
　　The hero Nature long had waited,
To read the secret of the sea,
　　To execute what God had fated ;
To fling the ocean's gates ajar,
　　As Jesus those which sin created ;
To be, like Him, a guiding star
　　Whose light still shineth unabated.

CHAPTER XXII.

AL MEZZOGIORNO.

LATE in the autumn of 1854 I left Florence, not forever, but to pass a winter in Rome and Naples, from whence to seek again my Etruscan paradise of Indolence. I had seen Sienna repeatedly, Pisa also, and Lucca, those three gems of Middle-age art and decayed historic glory. As the journey over land from Florence to Rome is, in winter, uncomfortable, and only passably interesting, I went to Leghorn by railroad, thence to Civita Vecchia by steamer, and thence in a diligence to the capital of the Cæsars. The approaches to Rome are nearly as desolate as those to Jerusalem. A fortnight before my passage through that misgoverned, doleful *campagna*, the diligence had been stopped, its passengers plundered, and the mail relieved of two thousand dollars. Consequently, the fat Irish priest, the sandy-haired Prussian artist, and the grave Italians, who, with myself, formed our company, were all on the look-out for brigands, ready to deliver at a moment's notice, but praying rather to be delivered. We were agreeably disappointed, therefore, at meeting nothing more rascally than an occasional patrolling Roman dragoon. A sick artilleryman of the garrison of Civita Vecchia, who was going home on leave, pointed to one of these really fine-looking troopers, and said, with a derisive smile, "All blackguards, *Signor*. They are in league with the robbers, and share profits with them."

"What are these brigands?" I asked him. "Are they regular bandits, who keep the mountains and live in caves, such as we see pictures of?"

"No, only peasants or shepherds, who rob by night, and follow their plows or their sheep the next day as if nothing had happened."

"Why does not the police ferret them out, then, since it could do it so easily?"

"Ah, *Signor*, you are a foreigner. They pay the police better than the government does."

I hope that no one expects me to say a word about the galleries of Rome, or the ruins, or the festas. I have undertaken to write a book about people, and I shall leave all those other wonders to some more diligent student of Murray's invaluable "Hand-book."

Making a tour of some of the better streets to find lodgings, I discovered that rooms were about twice as expensive and half as good in Rome as in Florence. Entering a house where chambers were advertised to let on the third floor, I stopped by mistake at the second, and rather surprised the respectable *padrona* by demanding quarters. It was a new idea to her; she had not placarded any hospitality for single gentlemen; but, now that one such offered himself, she was more charitable than I had found the nuns of Florence. Thus, before night, I was installed in two comfortable front rooms of a decent citizen's tenement on the Monte Pincio. Mine host was a well-educated, good-natured, broad-faced, pursy gentleman of fifty, an official in the Papal Mint. He often came into my parlor of an evening to pass an hour or so in reading poetry with me, discussing Italian literature, and repeating the news of Rome. "You are the first American," said he, "that I ever heard speak, and I like your accent exceedingly. Is it possible that your language is the same with the English? And yet you speak so differently! They talk just like birds, those English. They gabble our Italian all in their throats."

I believe it is true that our American accent in a foreign tongue is considerably different from that of an Englishman, although which is apt to be the most correct I would not undertake to decide, not even on the authority of mine host of the Monte Pincio.

He told me that once in a year all the officials of the government were treated to a kiss of the Pope's foot, and he described to me, with considerable vanity and appetite, his own participation in that ennobling enjoyment. "It is very clean," said he, speaking of the sacred pedal, "well washed beforehand, and raised on a cushion, so that we can get at it easily. Now the Pope, Pio Nono, was an old schoolfellow of mine, and he remembers it to this day. The very last time I kissed his foot he looked at me most graciously, and says he, 'Ah! Gigi' (that is me—that is my name); 'ah! Gigi,' says he, and smiled. Then he pointed to my mustaches; you know the Pope can not bear mustaches, because they are worn by Republicans. 'Ah! Gigi,' says he, 'I dislike those things.' 'Excuse me, your holiness,' says I, 'but I have been used to them from youth, and can not bear to part with them.'"

Perhaps, thought I, they tickled the sacred foot.

I found among the Romans a feeling of deep political dissatisfaction, not so much with the Pope personally as with the temporal government of the papacy.
They would like to see a republic or a constitutional
monarchy established throughout Italy, and Pio Nono
reduced to his proper position of a spiritual pontiff and
nothing more.   It was against the cardinals, and particularly against that master of priestcraft, Antonelli,
that they grumbled the most bitterly.   One man, a
person of the same respectable grade of society as my
landlord, told me that Antonelli was a great scoundrel,
and represented a family which had enriched itself by
connivance with the brigands who have always infest-
ed the frontier between Rome and Naples.   The same
gentleman said that there were thousands of people in
the public prisons who had not only been seized without any known accusation, but condemned and punished without trial.   Pointing out to me an interesting young woman of twenty-seven, leading a little
child, he informed me that her husband had lately
been kidnapped on pretense of some shadowy misde-
meanor committed twelve years before.   She had not
yet learned his real offense; she could not even discover where he was incarcerated; all she knew was
that he had not returned to her one night, and that the
police had told her not to search for him.

To speak jestingly of serious matters, the Romans
would do well to take a lesson from a certain small
dog who haunts their Piazza di Spagna.   But Sikes
was an English cur, not an Italian one, and though
runty, as well as troubled with a chronic limp, possessed the true British pluck equally with the true

British appetite. The great exploit of Sikes, and what chiefly wrought his fame among travelers, was an effort of dexterous and successful audacity in providing himself a dinner. Many Romans never prepare their meals at home, but have them sent ready cooked from the *trattorias*, borne in huge tin cases on the heads of porters. One afternoon Sikes met a porter thus laden, and followed him for some distance, snuffing the delicious odor of soup, beef, mutton, et cetera. Sikes was hungry, and the exercise made him hungrier, but the *trattoria* man took no charitable notice of him, and hurried on to his destination. What could a dinnerless dog do, under the circumstances, but set his teeth into one of the rascal's legs, and hold on until the blood came? While the surprised individual yelled and jumped, down came the tin case, bursting open with the shock, and scattering its savory entrails over the pavement. Sikes put his teeth into a beefsteak, and vanished down a side street into some asylum, where the beefsteak, as such, soon ceased to exist. This achievement spread his name far and wide among the *trattoria* porters, who ever after held him in mingled terror and detestation. As for him, as far as I could investigate his feelings, he looked on the whole dinnercarrying set with fierce contempt; and I have repeatedly observed him turn up his lip as one of them went by, and give vent to a little growl, which seemed to say, "I can manage those tin-headed fellows; call on me if a beefsteak is wanted."

Now let the Romans unanimously set teeth into the fat legs of their popes and cardinals, instead of kissing their ignominious toes, and they too will have their just share of the beefsteaks of Italy.　Still, they could not do it alone.　No, the Italians never can be free until they are united; and as for Italian unity, it is, thus far, the haziest of dreams.　I verily believe that the Florentines and Leghornese, for instance, despise each other about as heartily as they hate the Austrians; and I am inclined to allow that neither their contempt nor their hatred are very egregiously misplaced.

I consider both Rome and Naples inferior in general architectural beauty to Florence, although their palaces are larger, and their public buildings more numerous.　Both, however, far surpass in this respect any Anglo-Saxon city, and will do so, whatever our splendor may be, as long as we hold to our present method of planning private houses.　We divide our blocks vertically into small sections, each with its own scant flight of steps, its own trifling front door, its own stinted roof.　The consequence is a mean littleness of feature in our streets, a combination of narrow fronts, insignificant portals, brief ranges of windows, broken lines of cornice, and sudden, disagreeable contrasts of architecture.　The divisions in Europe are, on the contrary, horizontal, and the households reside, not in small separate dwellings, but in spacious stories.　This gives an opportunity to project vast edifices, continuous and imposing façades, noble portals, and a large, dignified style of ornament.　The buildings in Fifth Avenue are, perhaps, as costly as those on the Lung' Arno of Pisa; yet the former looks like a range of private tenements, while the latter has a stately palatial grandeur.　As for Broadway, it is at present, with all its riches, an architectural failure, and it would be necessary to line it with Astors and Metropolitans before it could rival the princely stateliness of the Roman Corso.

Aside from the vastly superior beauty attainable by this mode of building, there are social advantages in it which fully equal the advantages of our own method. "But," says Miss Caroline Pettitoes, "I do not desire *such* social advantages; I do not care, for instance, to know the family of that inevitable costermonger in the garret." My dear lady, do not annoy yourself with any such shocking supposition; you need not know the family in the attic any more than you need know the family in the porter's lodge at the great doorway. Go with your married brother to Florence, choose the street or the *piazza* which you like best, and hire a handsome apartment in one of those fine palaces that make the city glorious. You may live there a month, three months, six months, yet the stories above you and the stories below you shall still be to you a *terra incognita*. Through the superb arched portal, and up the broad, costly stairing you sweep at will, exchanging no glance of recognition with the people who meet you. The Italian marquis raises his hat because it is a lady who passes; but he no more speaks to you than your neighbor at home would address you on the Broadway pavement without an introduction. Consider further how very convenient for family purposes in New York would be this combination under one roof of apartments princely with apartments economical. At present your brother Howard, the merchant, lives a few blocks above Grace Church, while your brother John, the clerk, must seek his home four miles

off, somewhere above One Hundred and Fiftieth Street.
At Florence, Howard, John, yourself, your father and
mother (now too old to ride far), could all find abode,
according to their several means, on the different floors
of a noble palace, which should be called the Palazzo
Pettitoes.   Will your brother John say that he does
not care to receive notes and parcels directed to him in
the third story?   Ask him if he is not perfectly satisfied when he gets a chamber in the third story of the
St. Nicholas.   Custom makes the one genteel, tell
him, and custom could make the other genteel.

From Miss Pettitoes I return to the women of Rome,
concerning whom I will say that they appeared to me
the prettiest of Italy, and therefore the prettiest of Continental Europe.   As regular in feature as the *Fio-
rentina*, they have an expression of more fire, and forms
more lusciously developed.   It is to be confessed,
indeed, with sorrow, that, when a few years out of
girlhood, they become even too rounded and dim-
pled.

I consider the Italian women in general as not only
among the handsomest in the world, but as morally
admirable for true feminine nature.   They possess, in
an uncommon completeness, all the elements of perfect
womanliness : they are affectionate, constant, unsus-
picious, gentle-hearted, almost never coquettish, and
have that sweet timidity which we love in women.   I
say that nature has endowed them with these charming qualities ; I do not say that they always keep them
undesecrated by vices.   But if they are often false to
themselves and to others, who most deserves the
blame ?   Women are every where very much what

men make them; and if the husbands of Italy find their wives unfaithful, it is but the chastisement of their own libertinage. What astonishes one is the ever renewed confidence which the *Italiana* puts in her deceivers, after having been duped again and again. The last lover was a faithless monster, but the new one is sincere and adorable. There is no skepticism in her heart; she has an affectionate trustfulness that is beautiful. " Our women are very credulous," said a Palermitano to me; " tell them you love them, and they believe you immediately."

And then, replacing his cigar in his mouth, he nodded with a knowing, contemptuous air, as if he had stated one of the most ridiculous possible instances of infatuated simplicity. Well might he expect me to be stricken with wonder, for, in general, a more hypocritical set of gallants does not exist than the young men of Italy. A friend of mine, who, during a stay of some years in the country, has studied both people and language well, repeated to me a conversation illustrative of this subject. An English girl, residing at Florence to perfect herself in music, questioned him cautiously concerning a certain Signor Cavalloni, of that city.

" I know of him, at least," replied my narrator; " he is quite a beau here. Has he made your acquaintance ?"

" Made it ! he annoys me to death. That is just what I wished to consult you about. I want some one to keep him away from me."

" Indeed ! So you don't like him ?"

" Of course I don't. Why, he is extremely impudent. The other day he actually made me a regular declaration of love."

"Ah! that was a great piece of impertinence, certainly. Well, I hope there is no need of warning you. I presume you understand the folly of trusting these Italian gallants."

"I understand very well that he does not wish to marry me. But you should have seen him and heard him; you would certainly have thought that he was in love with me to distraction. He begged very hard to be allowed to sit down by me, or, at least, to take my hand. But I kept my fingers out of his reach, and stood bolt upright until he left. And then he talked—oh how movingly and mournfully he talked!"

"Did he cry?"

"Cry! why, you surprise me. How came you to suspect that he cried? I never meant to tell you that; I thought it was too absurd to be believed. Yes, he cried plentifully, copiously. But, now, what made you suppose that he cried?"

"Oh, they always fall back on their tears when matters look desperate. It is a famous resource with them, and very commonly used, I assure you."

"Dear me! I never knew before that it was a man's trick. Oh! I am vexed with him now, for he really deceived me, you know. I thought he was deeply in love when he cried, and I began to pity him. Well, if he pesters me again, I hope you will help me get rid of him."

"Of course, with the greatest pleasure. We will try our best to make him cry some more."

By way of closing this chapter, I shall offer a sketch of one of my lady acquaintances,

"Di quel bel passe là dove 'l si suona."

Her palace is a four-storied stone edifice of simple yet graceful fashion, with a carriage-entrance opening into the court, and balconies overlooking a square adorned by one of the finest churches of the city. I step within the arched portal, and ring at a lofty gate of strong latticed woodwork. It flies open at the tension of a cord drawn in some invisible servants' hall, and, as I enter a passage paved with broad flag-stones, closes behind me like the gate of an enchanted palace. No one appears thus far, for no one knows whether I intend to call on the lady of the first story or on her sister-in-law of the story above. I ascend a wide, handsome stairway of stone, and find myself on a spacious landing-place, where there is another door, much smaller than the one below, but still of brave dimensions and solidity. I ring, and a servant appears to answer my inquiry if the signora receives this afternoon. A *"Si, Signor,"* a bow, and a wave of the hand usher me into the hall, and from thence into an ante-room, at which point the liveried Giacomo disappears, knowing that I am acquainted with the apartments. I pass through a reception room with a vaulted ceiling and frescoed walls, lighted by a fine window which opens into one of the front balconies. I do not turn to the right into the great pictured saloon, because I am aware that it is only used on more stately occasions. A murmur of voices to the left guides me to the door of a charming boudoir, the walls of which are draped to the floor with blue silk, while the same delicate

stuff covers the chairs and divans.   The room is not
small in reality, but appears so from its comparative
loftiness.   In one corner of it—in the same corner
where I always find her on these receptions—sits the
lady of the house.   By the dim light which falls
through the heavily-curtained window I see a form,
slender almost to fragility, lounging with a voluptuous
indolence of posture and manner in an arm-chair massive and silken enough for a throne.   She has a pale
but perfectly clear complexion ; eyes long-lashed, and
black even to glitteringness ; dark, straight hair, braided
with an exquisite complexity ; features too aquiline for
a perfect contour, yet, on the whole, agreeable ; while
throughout the face dreams a refined languor, occasionally relieved by a flush of emotion.

A smile, half of conventional welcome, half perhaps
of real friendliness, salutes my entrance.   Next come
inquiries how I continue to like Florence, and whether
I have heard any thing amusing since we last parted ;
after which the signora turns again to the Countess de
Chalonge to recommence an interrupted conversation
on the expected ball of that evening at the Casa Nobile.
The countess describes the dress which she intends to
wear, and begs the same confidence of her rival.   The
latter, having depicted minutely her proposed flowers
and flounces, turns once more to me, demanding,
" Shall you be there to see me, Monsieur ?"

" No, Madame, but I shall pass the whole evening
in imagining you there."

This passionate response means nothing, and is a
mere triviality of politeness.   Still, it wins a good-
humored smile from my hostess, and a look of approval

from her lady visitor, who thinks, perhaps, that I have said a very genteel thing, considering that I am not a Frenchman. Presently the countess rises and takes her departure, saluting the *signora* with soft well-wishes and anticipations of a pleasurable meeting in the evening, but (as she amuses herself at present with an affectation of prudery) scarcely deigning to notice me in her rustling exit from the boudoir.

Now it is my turn, and I parade my best ideas on —no matter what—the Opera, the last new singer, the last new comedy, the races, balls—conversational knick-knacks, in short, of all descriptions. If we speak of poetry, my lady amateur almost invariably quotes Petrarch, for she is very sentimental, notwithstanding that she pretends to have seen through all this life's illusions. We are just in the middle of a sonnet, perhaps, when I hear steps in the outer room, and a brisk little marquis skips through the doorway. He compliments "Madame" in French, although he is a born Florentine, and, taking her hand, he touches it lightly to his lips. The action means nothing, or next to nothing, and is received without a blush or a look of surprise. According to Italian rules of courtesy, it is now my duty to go, and leave the field open to my successor. Informing the lady that I have the honor to bid her good-by, I bow myself out of the room, while she nods, smiles, and responds, if she cares to see me again soon, "*A bentosto*" (until very soon), or, perhaps, "*A dimane sera*" (until to-morrow evening).

Sometimes I met more people at these receptions; then the conversation became general, and every body talked to every body, acquainted or not. Rarely were persons presented to each other, as all were supposed for the time to be equals and friends, however strange they might be to each other the moment of their exit from the palace. This is better than our custom of universal introductions, and gives a freer movement to society in any chance reunion.

Once, when calling of an evening at an Italian house, I found quite a circle, including the husband and wife, both young, two sisters of the gentleman, and several visitors of both sexes. We were in the large dancing saloon, a fine room, with a lordly, arched ceiling, and frescoed walls decorated by pictures of real merit. The eldest sister, a gay, good-hearted creature, lively and boisterous for an Italian lady, sat down to the piano, and played the choicest parts of Robert the Devil. The others moved through a pantomime of that wild opera with a facility, a grace, and an expression which would have done honor to long artistic experience. Very unwillingly did I allow myself to be forced into the game, for I felt as if my northern stiffness jarred harshly with the flexile movement and power of personification instinctive in these southern natures. So let them fly away now from my memory, treading on skies of music and interwinding through a dance of poesy!

CHAPTER XXIII.

ACQUAINTANCE IN STONE.

THUS far I have only noted such of my European acquaintance as belonged to the biped or quadruped species. But man has other intimates than man in the world—others even than birds, beasts, fishes, insects, and reptiles. He is able so to vivify his own creations, so to impress them with his own thoughts and emotions, that they also are to a degree changed into living creatures, and stand for such to every educated sensitive spirit. The sculptor becomes not only the father of his own statue, but the relative of every other man's statue. He may not like his new nephews and cousins, indeed; he may regard them with jealousy, envy, contempt, hatred, and indifference; but he has married into the family for better or for worse; nor will the high-priest Nature ever grant him a divorce. And as the sculptor becomes kinsman to the marble people, so do the rest of us become its acquaintance. We fall in love with the Venus de Medici, pause with sympathy before the eternal suffering of the Laocoon, turn away from the face of the knife-grinder to wonder for years over its hidden yet earnest meaning, remember the Dying Gladiator with as much compassion as we remember the Byron who described him, forget not the sublime grace of the Apollo when the tourists who stood by our side before his pedestal have long since passed from our memory.

M

Nor is it the statue alone that thus becomes instinct with life to us. Pictures, temples, castles, palaces, the sites of fallen cities, a thousand things that have been touched by man, are blessed with some remnant of his life, and can often rise at our desire into living, sympathetic creatures, as the skeletons which the Prophet saw transformed themselves at his word into the warriors of an exceeding great army. The splendor of a perished empire may exhale visibly from a shattered vase or violated sarcophagus, as the Genii rose out of the brazen bottle before the eyes of the fisherman. Italy is crowded with the bones of history and with the relics of art, waiting but the passage of a poetic spirit to be clothed upon with a beautiful resurrection.

Into Italy, therefore, I entered as into a Valley of Vision, where I should behold glories little less than unutterable. Memorable and humiliating was my disappointment. Despite of strong effort to realize the historic value of the scenes around me, despite of dutiful pilgrimages to countless classic shrines, I remained the same being that I had been in America, the spirit equally clogged by the body, the wings of the imagination as easily wearied as ever, and the terrestrial nature which they have to upbear as ponderous.

More than this, the very beauty of Italy, the finish of its scenery, and the luxury of its climate, seemed to lap me into an unusual sensuousness of enjoyment. Particularly was this noticeable at Florence, where I staid longest and fought my earthliness hardest. I wondered how Galileo could have been intellectual there, how Dante and Michael Angelo could have been sublime there. It was in vain, for the most part, that I tried to study the art which was around me, or tried to call up the antiquity which crouched mysteriously behind it, and I returned forever to the starlight on the Arno, to the sunlight on the green hills, to the whispering groves of the Cascine, as to the immemorial and rightful deities of the locality.

Yet occasionally in Florence were there some uprisings of the famous past, especially when I halted to gaze at the aged battlements and beetling tower of the Palazzo Vecchio. Once more the Gonfaloniere swept through the portal; once more the trades and companies met in confused election; once more arose a discordant but free murmur of Guelf and Ghibelline voices. And then again suddenly all these visions melted into the indolent sunshine, or were borne away on the ripple of the *poco-curante* Arno. The experience of others may be magnificently different from this, but at least one fellow-traveler and travel-writer tells me that it was his story in Florence as well as mine.

In architecture, my most intimate friends while in the Tuscan capital were the old palaces and the Campanile of the Duomo. In the former I thought I could see the pugnacious vigor of the Florentine nobility in the days of Dante, combined with the industrial utility and elegant taste which marked it in the days of the Medici. Commencing with a story of rustic work solid and severe enough for a fortress, the mansions of the old merchant princes rise with an easy largeness of style, through several gradations of finish, tiara'd at last by a Corinthian cornice of audacious breadth and

exquisite design.   The Strozzi and the Riccardi particularly are models of this austerely beautiful palatial
architecture.

Yet even under such stately walls my wayward imagination refused to labor, and indolently went to sleep
in the Capuan present, unregardful as any basking laz-
zarone of the many pictures of history which it might
have conjured out of the venerable names and presences
of these monuments of mediæval princeliness, but gloat-
ing unweariedly on the masculine masses and multitudinous shadows of the rustic work, on the fine pro-
gression of finish as the edifice rose from story to
story, and on the daring yet graceful outspreading of
the rich Corinthian cornice.

The Campaniles of Italy are lofty and usually slender belfries, in some cases attached to the body of a
church, but in general standing a little apart, like an
angel who, with devout awe, sentinels some gate of
Paradise.   The Campanile of the Florentine Duomo
is worthy of this comparison, for its majesty is marvelous, and its beauty almost spiritual in delicacy, while
its bells seem like a seraph voice summoning earth at
morn to labor, and at night to holy meditation.   Only
when their clamor burst forth by my side, as I stood
in the dizzy gallery at the summit, did they convey to
me an impression of pain and terror ; for then the pile
appeared to shudder to its immense base under the
power of that brazen passion, as if it trembled with the
imprisoned agony of some mighty and condemned spirit, reminding me of that Afrite in the Arabian Nights
who was bound for uncounted years in an immeasurable pillar, from the pinnacle of which he shrieked to

the desert his mighty crime and his astonishing punishment.

But in general the impression left upon me by the
Campanile was that of the serenest and loveliest majesty.   Its style is Gothic, but so softened in outline,
so gentle in expression, that, for a time, you hardly notice its order of architecture.   Simple in form, a mere
quadrangular column, it is so delicately varied with
arches, pillarings, and statues, so superbly enameled
with many-colored marbles, that it fills the beholder
with a rare impression of richness and costliness.   It
is worthy of the age which produced the Divine Come-
dia.

The Duomo, at least in its exterior, never moved me
like its slender companion structure.   Its unfinished
front and its redundant ornament in the completed
portions detract from the grand effect produced by the
ponderous mass of the building and its daring dome.
But the interior, with its large spaces and stern simplicity, was always imposing; not in the hours of
service alone, when multitudes kneeled in the sublimity of numbers before a spangled splendor of worship,
but more particularly august in the desertion of twilight, when the shadows of the colonnades began to
mingle with the gloom of the hour itself, as the traces
of every purpose and desire within the human heart
finally disappear in the mystery of death.

The church of Santa Croce will remain longer in
my memory for the magic of a sunset which found
me within its walls.   A tender light fell through
the lofty windows, filling the dimness of the edifice
with a glory which was both sweet and very mourn-

ful.   I stood before the tomb of Michael Angelo when
I first became aware of the unearthliness of the scene
and the hour.   Above me was the bust of the great
master, beside which, contemplating his mausoleum,
sat the three sisters who loved him, Painting, Sculp-
ture, and Architecture.   Upon the faces of the statues
the sunset had poured the very soul of art, represent-
ing there a sorrow beyond the expressibilities of marble, a grief human yet most spiritual, resigned yet
which no words could have spoken ; an affliction growing ever more comfortless as the twilight · deepened
over the sculptured visages, until, at last, each sister
seemed ready to veil her head, and all night remain
covered in memory of her irreparable bereavement.

In the Via Calzaiuoli of Florence, midway between
the Piazza Gran-Duca and the Piazza of the Duomo,
rises the tower-like church of Or San Michele.   In a
niche of the exterior wall, shielded from the rain by a
marble canopy, stands a warrior with bare head, but
otherwise in complete armor.   With one mailed hand
upon his shield, with one foot advanced as if in defi-
ance of pagan and infidel, he rests an everlasting sen-
tinel, significant that the Church is yet militant, and
that there is no discharge in that war which he has
undertaken.   Multitudes walk before him by day on
the errands of peaceful labor, or wander near him by
night chanting the songs of worldly mirth, but he rec-
ognizes no companionship with them, and gazes passionately on something invisible to their eyes with a
fixed concentration of devout purpose, an unregarding
scorn of whatever is merely temporal, and an ineffable
hatred of whatever, temporal or eternal, is evil.   You

would expect to see this warrior leap clanging from his post, and fulfill immediately his martial yet holy mission, were it not that he is only of marble.   It is the St. George of Donatello, the statue before which Michael Angelo used to stand in wonder, and to which he cried "March!" in the thrill of his artistic sympathy.   Its form is rude compared with some more ancient and more modern statues, but its posé is noble, and its expression is more than human.

Of Michael Angelo himself there stands in the Piazza Gran-Duca one memorial, the statue of David, colossal by measurement, and equally so by its grandeur of feeling.   It rests on one leg, in easy confidence of success; its head is turned with a beautiful scorn to look at the approaching enemy; although the battle is yet to come, triumph already glorifies its forehead. A wonderful symbol of everlasting and heroic youth, it seemed to me also like an embodiment of Liberty, standing forward, naked and with simple weapons, to encounter the mailed giant Despotism.

No other colossal statue ever struck me as possessing the full nobleness of this.   There are critics, indeed, with brains made of foot-rules and compasses, who object that the hands are too big for the arms, the feet for the legs, and the head for the body.   I reply, that in youth the extremities are always larger in relation to the other parts than when the frame has reached its full development; and, even if it were not so, I observe the fierce, sublime soul of the statue, and forget every slight disproportion in the form which clothes it.

Less heroic, more ethereal, the expression of agile

grace stands, or almost soars, the Mercury of Giovanni di Bologna.   With one foot barely touching the
pedestal, with its confident brow turned toward heav-
en, it reminds one of all swift and untrammeled things
—of winds bounding over tree-tops, of sunlight dancing
on the pinnacles of spires, of tireless clouds launching
from the summits of mountains.   Could there be any
better statuesque representation of the elasticity and
unweariableness of the true artist's imagination ?   If
it is not, as I think it, the finest of all Mercuries, ancient
or modern, it is at least the chiefest glory of Giovanni
di Bologna.

Canova moved me to a sudden but transient admiration.   His forms and groupings are extremely graceful, but he has nowhere produced, as it seems to me, a
complete nobleness of expression.   His beautiful Per-
seus is too mere an echo of the Apollo Belvidere, and
his female faces are disappointing by their insipidity.

A greater and more original artist is the living Roman Tenerani, a disciple of the pure Thorwaldsen, but
not bound to him by any link of slavish imitation ; a
master of originality, of loveliness, of chastity in line,
of holiness in feeling.   In the church of San Giovanni
Laterano, in the Torlonia chapel, I saw his Descent
from the Cross.   Simplicity of grouping, mournful
tenderness of expression, sinless spirituality of sentiment, have no diviner union in art.   It reminded me
of the seraphic sweetness far withdrawn from earth, the
peace which passeth all understanding, which beam
from the pictures of Fra Beato Angelico.

In a chamber near the Palace Barberini in Rome I
beheld an angel clothed in robes like the driven snow.

Of gigantic stature, he sat in an attitude of expectation on a white and glittering throne. In his hand he held a trumpet, ready to summon earth to judgment, and to declare that time should be no longer. His face was that of one who had seen all human and heavenly mysteries, yet was beautiful with the freshness of everlasting youth. It was the Angel of the Last Judgment of Tenerani.

It will easily be guessed why I do not go on to call up gods and goddesses from the vasty deep of ancient art. That ocean is immeasurable to an ordinary pinnace, and those shapes are terrible to an inexperienced mariner.

I was disappointed in the nature of my emotions at Florence, but I was disappointed in their quantity at Rome. The Imperial City did not satisfy me, partly because during my stay it was clouded, inclement, and uncomfortable with winter, but chiefly because I anticipated most there some glorious spectral resurrection of the past, and there had most reason to complain of my imagination. I thought that under the Arch of Titus and on the Flaminian Way I should hear the tramp of legionaries. I expected on the Hill of the Capitol to see august shades pass by in consular robes. But arches and ways had none of the echoes for which I listened; and, like most others, I found the Capitoline vacant, except of tourists, guides, and beggars.

I must speak thankfully, however, of some memorable visits which I was enabled to make to the Pantheon. The same as in the days of the Cæsars, and yet how changed! still a temple, and yet with what a different worship! It was this continuation of the an-

M 2

cient sentiment of the building, contrasted with the immense variation in the direction of that sentiment, which startled me, and made me return many times to the Pantheon.

One other classic hour was accorded to me under earth, wandering among the tombs of the Scipios. It was astonishing to stand before those rude memorial tablets, and read, as they were written in the elder days, the names of Publius, and Cneius, and Nasica. My modernism seemed to disappear before their solemn magic, and I became a countryman of the old patricians, a client perhaps, and at least a mourner at their graves. The original stones, indeed, had been removed to the Vatican, and their place supplied by imitations ; but, not knowing this fact at the time, I passed just as fine an hour.

CONCLUSION.

AND here I might outpour an endless prattle
   About high art, and scenery, and song,
Or heroes' graves, or fields of ancient battle,
   Or broken fanes which to old gods belong;
But I shall not; my forte is tittle-tattle
   Concerning living men, the motley throng
Which greets the tourist's lazy observation
In street, and shop, and coach, and railway station.

I threaded Pompeii in wordless wonder,
   Its temples, theatres, and rutted ways,
Exactly as Vesuvius's judgment thunder
   Had flung them from antique to modern days;
But I received a caution not to blunder
   Into a long account of my surveys;
For, standing by an altar, with his fingers
Upon his lips, the God of Silence lingers.

I understood him, and so leave the story
   Of Pompeii in Bulwer Lytton's hand;
I pass with equal self-command the hoary
   Solemnity of Pestum, lonely-grand,
Although to me it wore the finest glory
   Of any ruin in Italic land:
A massive glory, Greek—yea, Magna Grecian,
Which Remus might have seen in full completion.

My right as tourist to the population
   Of gods and muses in the Vatican,
To all the picture-galleries in creation,
   To every monument yet built by man,
To all the glaciers of the Switzer nation,
   To holy spots from Beersheba to Dan,
To Lago Como and the Milan Duomo,
I here resign to any other *homo*.

Resigning, too, my pen, I stop this babble
　　Respecting my acquaintance and myself;
For though, perhaps, an interesting rabble,
　　The theme is spent: I lay it on the shelf;
Sadly uncertain if my pribble-prabble
　　Will bring me notoriety or pelf,
But pretty sure at least of being printed,
As several bookish friends have kindly hinted.

THE END.

By William C. Prime.

Boat Life in Egypt & Nubia.

Boat Life in Egypt and Nubia. By WILLIAM C. PRIME, Author of "The Old House by the River," "Later Years," &c. Illustrations. 12mo, Muslin, $1 25.

Tent Life in the Holy Land.

By WILLIAM C. PRIME, Author of "The Old House by the River," "Later Years," &c. Illustrations. 12mo, Muslin, $1 25.

The Old House by the River.

By WILLIAM C. PRIME, Author of the "Owl Creek Letters." 12mo, Muslin, 75 cents.

Later Years.

By WILLIAM C. PRIME, Author of "The Old House by the River." 12mo, Muslin, $1 00.

LOSSING'S PICTORIAL FIELD-BOOK

Of the Revolution; or, Illustrations, by Pen and Pencil, of the History, Biography, Scenery, Relics, and Traditions of the War for Independence. 2 vols. Royal 8vo, Muslin, $8 00; Sheep, $9 00; Half Calf, $10 00; Full Morocco, $15 00.

A new and carefully revised edition of this magnificent work is just completed in two imperial octavo volumes of equal size, containing 1500 pages and 1100 engravings. As the plan, scope, and beauty of the work were originally developed, eminent literary men, and the leading presses of the United States and Great Britain, pronounced it one of the most valuable historical productions ever issued.

The preparation of this work occupied the author more than four years, during which he traveled nearly ten thousand miles in order to visit the prominent scenes of revolutionary history, gather up local traditions, and explore records and histories. In the use of his pencil he was governed by the determination to withhold nothing of importance or interest. Being himself both artist and writer, he has been able to combine the materials he had collected in both departments into a work possessing perfect unity of purpose and execution.

The object of the author in arranging his plan was to reproduce the history of the American Revolution in such an attractive manner, as to entice the youth of his country to read the wonderful story, study its philosophy and teachings, and to become familiar with the founders of our Republic and the value of their labors. In this he has been eminently successful; for the young read the pages of the "Field-Book" with the same avidity as those of a romance; while the abundant stores of information, and the careful manner in which it has been arranged and set forth, render it no less attractive to the general reader and the ripe scholar of more mature years.

Explanatory notes are profusely given upon every page in the volume, and also a brief biographical sketch of every man distinguished in the events of the Revolution, the history of whose life is known.

A Supplement of forty pages contains a history of the *Naval Operations of the Revolution*; of the *Diplomacy*; of the *Confederation* and *Federal Constitution*; the *Prisons* and *Prison Ships of New York*; *Lives of the Signers of the Declaration of Independence*, and other matters of curious interest to the historical student.

A new and very elaborate analytical index has been prepared, to which we call special attention. It embraces eighty-five closely printed pages, and possesses rare value for every student of our revolutionary history. It is in itself a complete synopsis of the history and biography of that period, and will be found exceedingly useful for reference by every reader.

As a whole, the work contains all the essential facts of the early history of our Republic, which are scattered through scores of volumes often inaccessible to the great mass of readers. The illustrations make the whole subject of the American Revolution so clear to the reader that, on rising from its perusal, he feels thoroughly acquainted, not only with the history, but with every important locality made memorable by the events of the war for Independence, and it forms a complete Guide-Book to the tourist seeking for fields consecrated by patriotism, which lie scattered over our broad land. Nothing has been spared to make it complete, reliable, and eminently useful to all classes of citizens. Upward of THIRTY-FIVE THOUSAND DOLLARS were expended in the publication of the first edition. The exquisite wood-cuts, engraved under the immediate supervision of the author, from his own drawings, in the highest style of the art, required the greatest care in printing. To this end the efforts of the publishers have been directed, and we take great pleasure in presenting these volumes as the best specimen of typography ever issued from the American press.

The publication of the work having been commenced in numbers before its preparation was completed, the volumes of the first edition were made quite unequal in size. That defect has been remedied, and the work is now presented in two volumes of equal size, containing about 780 pages each.

Harper's New Catalogue.

A NEW DESCRIPTIVE CATALOGUE OF HARPER & BROTHERS' PUB-LICATIONS is now ready for distribution, and may be obtained gratuitously on application to the Publishers personally, or by letter enclosing SIX CENTS in postage stamps.

The attention of gentlemen, in town or country, designing to form Libraries or enrich their literary collections, is respectfully invited to this Catalogue, which will be found to comprise a large proportion of the standard and most esteemed works in English Literature—COMPREHENDING MORE THAN TWO THOUSAND VOLUMES—which are offered in most instances at less than one half the cost of similar productions in England.

To Librarians and others connected with Colleges, Schools, etc., who may not have access to a reliable guide in forming the true estimate of literary productions, it is believed the present Catalogue will prove especially valuable as a manual of reference.

To prevent disappointment, it is suggested that, whenever books can not be obtained through any bookseller or local agent, applications with remittance should be addressed direct to the Publishers, which will be promptly attended to.

Franklin Square, New York.

/

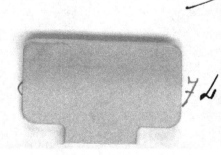

CPSIA information can be obtained
at www.ICGtesting.com
Printed in the USA
BVHW091901220819
556561BV00021B/4987/P